MW00468559

BACKPACKING
WITH CHILDREN

How to Go Lightweight, Have Fun,
and Stay Safe on the Trail

Malia Maunakea

The Colorado Mountain Club Press
Golden, Colorado

Backpacking with Children: How to Go Lightweight, Have Fun, and Stay Safe on the Trail
© 2023 Malia Maunakea

Published by:
The Colorado Mountain Club Press
710 10th Street, Suite 200, Golden, CO 80401
(303) 996-2743 | cmcpress@cmc.org | cmc.org/books

Founded in 1912, The Colorado Mountain Club is the largest outdoor recreation, education, and conservation organization in the Rocky Mountains. Look for our books at your local bookstore or outdoor retailer, or online at cmc.org/books.

Corrections: We greatly appreciate when readers alert us to errors or outdated information by emailing cmcpress@cmc.org.

Casey Blaine: editor
Vicki Hopewell: design and composition

Cover photo: Rae, Kaleo, and Malia on the Tahoe Rim Trail. Photo by David Heinrich

Distributed to the book trade by:
Mountaineers Books
1001 SW Klickitat Way, Suite 201, Seattle, WA 98134
(800) 553-4453 | mountaineersbooks.org

We gratefully acknowledge the financial support of the people of Colorado through the Scientific and Cultural Facilities District of greater metropolitan Denver for our publishing activities.

Printed in Korea

ISBN 978-1-937052-87-4

23 24 25 / 10 9 8 7 6 5 4 3 2 1

WARNING AND DISCLAIMER
Read, Enjoy, and Proceed at your own Risk

OUTDOOR RECREATION IS HAZARDOUS AND CAN EVEN BE DANGEROUS AND LIFE-THREATENING. Weather and terrain conditions can change often, rapidly, and unpredictably. Techniques, routes, and equipment change and evolve, and in the case of equipment, can wear out or break. Participant skills, abilities, and physical conditioning can also change or be inadequate for weather and terrain. The users or readers of this and all other Colorado Mountain Club ("CMC") books, articles, videos, and websites are solely responsible for their own safety, including using common sense and fully understanding their own knowledge, skills, abilities, equipment, surroundings, and conditions, and proceed at their own risk.

The information in this and all other CMC books, articles, videos, and websites is general in nature; discrepancies may exist between the text and the trails or routes in the field. Land managers may change, alter, or close trails. Check with local land management agencies before proceeding to receive the latest information and warnings.

HIKING, BACKCOUNTRY TRAVEL, MOUNTAINEERING, ALPINE CLIMBING, BACKCOUNTRY SKIING, ROCK CLIMBING, BOULDERING, ICE CLIMBING, AND OTHER MOUNTAIN AND OUTDOOR RECREATIONAL ACTIVITIES ARE DANGEROUS AND MAY RESULT IN SEVERE AND/OR PERMANENT INJURY OR DEATH. The user of the information contained in this publication assumes all risks of the use and application of the information provided or discussed within it.

The authors and CMC expressly disclaim all liability arising out of or related to the content of this and all other CMC books, articles, videos, and websites. The authors and publishers make no representations or warranties, express or implied, of any kind regarding the contents of these publications. All representations and warranties, express or implied, regarding this and all other CMC books, articles, videos, and websites and the accuracy of the information therein and the results of the use thereof are expressly disclaimed, including but not limited to any and all warranties of Merchantability and Fitness for a Particular Purpose.

CONTENTS

Rae, Dave, and Kaleo backpacking in the Porcupine Mountains, Michigan.

Introduction

ADVENTURING WITH KIDS

Taking my first steps on the 2,650-mile-long Pacific Crest Trail (PCT) as a 24-year-old newlywed in April 2006, after years of planning with Dave, my husband, was the most audacious thing I'd ever done. Until that point, I'd gone on just a handful of back-packing trips in my life, including a ridiculously hard 100-miler where I found myself crying and actually saying, "If labor is worse than this, I'm never having kids!"

That particular trip was a backpacking outing aimed at help-ing us train for the rigors of the PCT, and Dave had upped the ante to test our mettle. Things hadn't gone quite as planned, and we'd gotten lost, gone over the wrong pass, and were attempt-ing to scoot down a steep snowfield in order to get to the trail we could see below us. I was scared of heights so was on all fours crab-walking down the slope. My hands had gone numb; the thin gloves I was wearing were completely soaked through. Afterward, the pain of my palms regaining feeling had me crying as I sat in the mud below the snowfield.

That was the last training backpacking trip we did before setting foot on the PCT. Not exactly a confidence builder, but it sparked something in me. Once we were done and safely back in our climate-controlled house, I found myself reminiscing on the natural beauty in those particularly hard-to-reach places and the challenge it had been to get there. Dang, I was proud of us for what we'd done! I wanted to do it again. I couldn't wait for the Pacific Crest Trail. It seemed like the iconic long-distance trail would be our ultimate test.

About 900 miles into the PCT trip, on a bright, early morning in the High Sierra, Dave and I heard a loud, distinct "*Roar!*" that sounded more human than animal. Walking on, we began to hear the sounds of singing and laughing, and soon a family composed of parents and three daughters came into view.

We stopped and exchanged pleasantries. Dave asked if they had heard the roar earlier. The dad laughed and explained that's how they start their mornings before setting out to hike. This family was on the John Muir Trail (the PCT follows the same trail for about 170 miles) and had hiked the JMT every year since their youngest daughter was a wee little thing. Those girls looked like they were having a blast! It got me thinking.

Dave and I had the "Do you want children?" discussion a number of times while dating. We had agreed that growing our family was not going to happen, thinking that our lives were going to be filled with adventure and that kids would only hold us back. But one thing about hiking a long-distance trail is that you have a lot of time to think. And for the next 1,750 miles, I thought about

Our first backpacking trip as a family! Dave is carrying his old external-frame backpack that he has had since his Boy Scouting days because we could strap the kids' sleeping bags to the exterior. Rae was 4, and Kaleo was 2.5 (Golden Gate Canyon State Park, Colorado).

family. I pondered what adventure looked like to me. I talked to Dave about our life goals and plans for the future. Slowly a new picture began to form in my mind. For the first time, it seemed like there didn't have to be two separate life paths. Maybe our love of wild adventure and a desire to raise children could some-how coexist in our future. Many more miles and discussions later, we had made the decision. We were going to try to have kids.

We finished our PCT thru-hike on September 30, 2006. Our daughter was born the following summer and our son a few years after that.

As new parents, we were excited to get back into the woods and eager to share what we loved with our young family. We are lucky to live in Colorado where there are ample opportunities for outdoor play, and for a while, we were satisfied with car camping and taking amazing day hikes with our babies and toddlers. The backcountry was calling, though, so with a bit more planning, we took our first backpacking trip as a family of four in 2012, when our son was 2.5 and able to walk the 1.5-mile trail to the campsite on his own.

That's where it all began. At this point, our kids have hiked hundreds of miles, including a 170-mile backpacking trip around the Tahoe Rim Trail when they were 9 and 6. I'm not writing this to brag—other kids have definitely hiked farther at younger ages. I simply want to establish what my experience is. Dave and I have taken Wilderness First Aid and CPR classes, but I'm primarily writing to you as a mom with knowledge that comes from having a plethora of trail miles under her boots and conversations with other parents and experts along the way. This book is sprinkled with anecdotes from our family's adventures and lessons learned and is primarily geared toward families with children who are old enough to be potty trained, able to walk on their own, and sharing meals with the adults. For us, that was age two-and-a-half through the teen years.

Before we get started, I highly recommend you look into Wilderness First Aid or other outdoor safety classes in your area. The peace of mind that comes with knowing you're as prepared as possible when heading out with children is priceless. See the "Helpful Resources" section at the end of this book for ideas and more information.

WHY BACKPACK WITH KIDS?

Once upon a time in 2016, we were finishing up day eleven of a fifteen-day backpacking trip on the Tahoe Rim Trail. There had been steep ascents, tricky footing, and some snowy passes. The scenery had been gorgeous, but we were all tired and hungry. Dave and I finally found a spot to cook dinner that was relatively snow-free and shielded from the wind. With a massive exhale, I dropped my pack and sat, resting my tired body from the accumulated exertions of the last week. And then giggles and squeals of delight hit my ears. Smiling, I turned to see my kids, pack-free, sliding down a small snowbank next to me, and then climbing back up only to slide back down again. They were taking turns to see who could slide the silliest, taking running leaps, then going backwards, laughing, and playing together far better than they ever do at home, where life can get busy with appointments and other distractions and interferences. *This* is why we backpack.

The decision to immerse yourself in nature, with or without kids, can be both exhilarating and daunting. Whether planning for a weekend trip or a multimonth thru-hike, good backpackers meticulously research and plan what they will need when the going gets interesting. Adding children to the equation creates another level of unknown, sure, but it also opens up the opportunity for a special kind of magic.

Kids find joy in the simplest of things, and your own wonder will be rekindled when experiencing backpacking through the eyes of your child. Of course, it's not all joy and rainbows, but hopefully this book will help you keep the impacts of the inevitable thunderstorms—both mental and literal—to a minimum.

Whether you always knew you'd be taking your kids with you on your adventures or if you're just coming to realize that this path is an option, I'm here to help guide your family further into the great outdoors to experience the freedom and beauty that comes with going wild in nature.

In today's fast-paced world, it is increasingly difficult to truly unplug and unwind. We have computers on our desks, in our pockets, and on our wrists buzzing and dinging all day long, and our kids are plugging in as well. They have access to seemingly limitless amounts of programming and video games on the TV and the Internet. There is a time and place for that connection in the modern world, but the great news is that nature is there for us when we need to get away from it all.

In Richard Louv's book *Last Child in the Woods: Saving Our Children from Nature-Deficit Disorder,* he writes, "Unlike television, nature does not steal time; it amplifies it." His research suggests that when kids are removed from nature, they use their senses less, have attention difficulties, have more weight struggles, and have a greater chance of experiencing other emotional and physical illnesses. It also suggested that kids don't care as much about nature when they don't have as much exposure to it.

Rae soaking it all in on the Teton Crest Trail, Wyoming. Photo by David Heinrich

Time outdoors is the medicine we are learning we need. What's more, backpacking with our kids helps us reconnect with what is most important: each other. The whole family relies on each other for entertainment and camaraderie. When we stop for a snack break, our kids will sometimes start collecting sticks to build tiny forts together, or they pretend to make medicine together, or we all laugh at the crazy songs that Dave makes up and come up with additional verses together. Key word here is *together*. This sort of togetherness doesn't happen quite as organically or last as long when we are at home and everyone has other options.

Out in nature, you are able to focus on the most basic tasks, and everything becomes relatively clear and simple: you need

Benefits of Backpacking with Kids

Need some more motivation to get out on the trail with kids? Here are some of the many benefits of backpacking with kids:

▶ You can experience a lifetime of affordable family vacations once you have the gear (and the initial gear setup can be cheaper than a family vacation involving hotels, restaurants, and gas).

▶ Kids get to be kids. They can be loud and messy, eat with their hands, play in the dirt, and sit on the ground. There is less of a need for social graces, which leads to a certain sense of relaxation for everyone.

▶ It is pretty. Gorgeous. Breathtaking. You will likely see things that only folks willing to make the effort ever get to see. Maybe you'll see unusual wildflowers or unexpected wildlife. Whatever it is, it'll be memorable. What's more, your trip will be different from everyone else's.

▶ It's great for your health. Breathing clean air, stretching your legs, and moving your body gets your heart pumping and releases endorphins, the natural chemicals that increase feelings of happiness and reduce pain. Some doctors are even starting to prescribe time in nature as a benefit to mental and physical health!

▶ The connection you'll build with your kids away from tech and distractions is incredible. Memories of the good, bad, and ridiculous things that happen—and they will!—

will provide fodder for dinner-table discussions for years to come.

▸ Kids learn important life skills on the trail, everything from hygiene to food rationing to working through boredom to introspection. Not to mention all the lessons that nature provides, from weather patterns to flora and fauna.

▸ The simplicity of life on the trail benefits everyone. It gets you back to basics: one foot in front of the other, staying fed and hydrated, then going to sleep. Everything you need is on your back. It's amazing to remind yourself (and your kids) from time to time just how simple human needs can be.

▸ I've said it before and I'll say it again—backpacking as a family gets you focused on what is important: being together.

to eat, drink, sleep, and move from point A to point B without doing too much damage to your body. That's it! That's all that is involved. As long as you have what you need to accomplish those tasks for everyone in your party, you can backpack. Once those four needs are met, you're able to turn your extra energy toward your family and surroundings and simply take it all in.

OK, maybe it seems like I'm oversimplifying it a bit, but once you get out there and start putting one foot in front of the other, you'll find that you're free to let your mind wander until your kids call your attention back to them. And trust me, they'll call your attention back to them. Maybe they'll want to talk (for hours and hours, for days on end) about what they want for their next birthday—which is over six months away—or they'll want you to tell them a story or to tell you a story. Go with it. Talk it out.

Make sure you have a lot of water, as all of this bonding and communicating is thirsty work! Other times they'll get your attention because they are hot, tired, bored, thirsty, hungry, or cold. Dave and I always remind ourselves that they complain just as much at home (especially when they aren't on screens) and that whatever they are complaining about eventually passes.

In this book, you'll find out some ways to head off these common complaints in Chapter 11, "Games and Rewards." But remember, dealing with a sense of boredom or discomfort is a life skill and is easier to master in nature where there are so many distractions that stimulate your senses and imagination. And that's just one of the benefits.

Ready to dive in and learn a bit about what you need to start your own adventure? This book is divided into several parts, with information to help you get out on the trail as quickly as possible. Part 1 is filled with information for planning your trip. It will help you figure out the first steps: the basic when, where, how (permits and reservations), and food planning. Part 2 will go over prep and address gear. Part 3 is when you get to move! You'll figure out distances, campsite selections, and review the crucial principles of Leave No Trace. Part 4 is all about fun and games, discussing delights such as food and drink on the trail, along with games and reward systems. Finally, Part 5 is about anticipating and overcoming obstacles that may arise.

GOING LIGHTWEIGHT

You may have heard a lot of buzz about lightweight backpacking. It's become increasingly popular to lighten the load, allowing you to hike farther and faster. Is "going lightweight" really that big of a deal? Or is it a just jargony buzzword thrown in to help sell more expensive gear? What does it even mean? And is it possible with kids?

Making the commitment to "go lightweight" is something my husband and I did for our PCT thru-hike. It started when Dave's mom gifted him Ray Jardine's book *Beyond Backpacking.* Jardine's reasons for going light struck a chord with us. At the heart of his philosophy was that having a lighter-weight pack meant he was able to go more miles more easily. His body didn't hurt as much, he didn't expend as much energy, and he was able to carry less food between resupply points because he covered the distance in fewer days, which led to an even lighter pack.

Dave and I followed a lot of Jardine's advice, even going so far as trimming off half of our toothbrush handles at one point, before recalibrating and finding a happy medium. My knees and shoulders have never been great (my shoulder used to hurt just carrying my clarinet in marching band in high school), so I am sure that lightening our packs made the completion of the PCT possible. Over the past two decades, we have crafted a lightweight system that has worked for our family.

Being as comfortable as possible while backpacking is a huge goal, especially with kids who live their lives like *The Princess and the Pea*, where every out-of-place rub is potentially hike-stopping. By making intentional decisions about what to put in your packs, you can limit the aches on your body. No one likes lugging a painful amount of weight around, and I can pretty much guarantee your kids won't fully appreciate the beauty of the great outdoors if they're encumbered by what they deem an outrageous load.

So, what does it actually mean to go lightweight? The answer lies in a pack's base weight: the weight of the pack fully loaded without food, water, or fuel. Lightweight packs have a base weight of under 20 pounds, and ultralightweight packs are under 10 pounds. Over the years, our adult-pack base weights have fluctuated from right around that 10-pound mark to somewhere closer to 15 pounds when hiking with kids (additional tent, bear bags, etc.). In this book, I hope to help educate you on the plethora of options out there and help you make informed decisions when purchasing gear. Most of my suggestions will help you easily fall into the lightweight category.

Take a close look at your "Big Three" gear items (detailed in Chapter 3), and don't stop there. Question everything you put in your pack. Is there a lighter alternative or a piece of gear you're already carrying that will do? It's not that you have to spend a ton of money getting the latest and greatest in scientific advancements. Just be conscious of every choice. Ounces add up to pounds. And pounds add up to pain.

Avoid bulky and heavy gear as much as possible. Yes, lighter gear tends to be made with fewer layers or more delicate fabric, but with a bit of education and training, your kids can learn to treat lightweight gear with enough respect and care that it can withstand the test of time, toddlers, and trail miles.

There is a synergy to developing your lightweight system, a sort of symbiotic relationship between your gear, your pack, your shoulders, your feet, and your whole body. Same goes for your kids' gear. If you make the effort to keep things light, your body will have to do less work to carry your pack. This means you will have extra energy to walk farther, or faster, or both. Or you can just stroll along leisurely and take time to smell the roses without wanting to take your pack off for a break every five minutes. The kids will want to smell the roses anyway. Having a lighter pack makes it easier to focus on the journey, not the effort.

As backpackers like to say, "Hike your own hike." While I hope the advice in this book resonates with you, the main thing is to get out into nature together—however you want to do it— and enjoy the moments.

PLAN

Design the Trip

THERE ARE LOTS OF websites, blogs, and books with glossy images of smiling families in the middle of some magnificent wild area. Some families are even brave enough to show a few less-than-ideal photos of trouble they ran into on an adventure. We have an amazing picture of gap-toothed Kaleo holding a pine cone the size of his head against his cheek on one of our trips. He named it Bob and loved said pine cone, hiking with it for 11 miles, telling it stories, and playing with it during breaks. Unfortunately, 3 miles after a bathroom break, Kaleo realized he no longer had Bob. We told him he could not go back to get him as it would add 6 miles to our day. Oh, the tears! It was *the worst*. I tried to ease his pain by reminding him that we have a wonderful picture of Bob, and that he wouldn't have been able to take him out of that park anyway due to Leave No Trace (never miss an opportunity to reinforce these values). He eventually accepted that Bob was

Dave, Rae, and Kaleo backpacking in the Porcupine Mountains, Michigan.

gone for good, and when we got home, he loved that I put the picture of him with Bob in the family album.

Behind the photo album lies not only a lot of great stories, but let's face it, a whole lot of planning. Sometimes a year or more of work goes into a single trip, depending on the itinerary. But you know how to climb Mount Everest, right? One step at a time.

The Internet, books, and outdoor stores are full of inspiration. Search various hashtags (try #familybackpacking and #backpackingfamily as examples) to find other families out there doing their thing across the country and even around the world. Have your kids with you as you look at pictures of trails and areas you'd love to visit. If you have friends who like to hike and camp, go on adventures with them as a warm-up (and see if they'd be interested in joining you on a backpacking trip).

One thing we try to avoid is asking the kids if they *want* to go backpacking. We don't want to risk them saying no! But depending on their age, they can be involved in other parts of planning by giving them options. For example, ask if they want to do a loop or an out-and-back, or show them pictures of highlights from different trails and ask which they'd like to see more. Ask if they prefer pasta or stir-fry the first night, or if they'd rather bring their toy truck or their toy dinosaur. When kids feel included and even consulted, they are more likely to view the trip positively and with excitement.

Planning your trip also involves answering the following key questions:

- ▸ **Where:** How far from home will you travel, and how long of a trip will it be?
- ▸ **When:** When will you go, and how will that timing impact your preparation?
- ▸ **How:** What permits and/or reservations, if any, does backpacking in your chosen area involve?
- ▸ **Food:** Good food and happy stomachs are key to any backpacking trip with kids. What food (and how much) should you bring on your adventure? Start planning out meals and snacks as soon as you know your where, when, and how.

This part of the book is all about the not-always-pretty-but-always-necessary nitty-gritty background information and research required for a great trip. We are diving into the behind-the-scenes stuff that glossy magazine pictures and adventure websites don't typically show. Because in order to be successful out there, the work comes first. So, let's get started.

WHERE WILL YOU GO? DESTINATIONS, ROUTES, AND MAPS

From choosing where in the world you will hike to plotting out specifics, such as where you will set up your tent each night, dialing in on your "where" is key to any successful trip. Getting these details organized as thoroughly as possible will help your family enjoy their time in the outdoors. I will talk more about campsite reservations later in this chapter, but for now, let's consider the big, broad questions you need to settle.

For starters, figure out how to get to the start of your hike and how far in you will need to hike on the first day in order to set up your tent. Knowing this information will help you calculate what time everyone needs to be fully packed and ready to leave home to ensure you can set up your tent before dark. If you are driving to the trailhead, plan out your parking options. Know if permits are necessary to leave your vehicle for multiple nights. If your travel plans involve flying or other mass transit, research what can be carried on versus checked through or mailed ahead to your destination. Things that could raise red flags include pocketknives, trekking poles, and liquids (including fuel).

Trail Types

Next, decide what kind of trail you're looking for. Different trail options include out-and-backs, loops and lollipops, and point-to-points. An out-and-back trip means seeing new trail for half of the trip, then turning around and returning on that same trail all the way back to the car. A fun game on an out-and-back hike is to have your kids look for identifiable markers on the way out, such as big trees, unusual boulders, or streams. Then on the way back, make it a game to look for those same markers and remember what should be coming up next and how many more are left. You can also teach them the navigation skill of looking back at your trail to make it easier to recognize on the hike home!

A loop trail gives you the opportunity to see new things the entire trip. Sometimes there is a short out-and-back section that you need to hike in order to get to the loop. Your kids may like knowing that this is often called a lollipop (think of it as a loop on a stick). When you finish the loop, you simply hike back along the "stick" to your car to end the adventure.

A third option is a point-to-point hike, which is a little more logistically complicated. You start the hike from one location and end somewhere else. The pro is that, similar to a loop, the trail is new every step of the way. No backtracking or repeats. The con is that you have to figure out transportation. If you leave your car at the start, then you will need to get back to your car when the hike is over. Options might include bus, taxi, hitchhiking, or a friend willing to pick you up and drive you back to the starting point. Or you can park your car at the finish, find a ride to the start, and hike back to your car, which is what we like to do. You can also bring two cars on the trip, leaving one at the destination and then shuttling to the start line; after the hike, you pick up your other car. What's nice about doing it this way is that when you're done, you instantly have the comfort of your own vehicle and the ability to leave right away, no matter what time.

Terrain and Mileage

Planning where to go also includes investigating the terrain. Gather maps of your options. Consult online resources such as AllTrails, Hiking Project, CalTopo, or blogs. Once you've chosen an area, it is wise to also pick up physical maps, which you can carry with you on your trip. Learn to read topography (topo) maps, so you get a better understanding of what the trail will feel like when elevation lines are close together versus farther apart or when the trail ventures above tree line or crosses water.

Knowing your family's rough pace, use these maps to estimate how far you could walk in a day and if that mileage will result in you being on a cliff with steep slopes (tight elevation lines) or a flat area in a valley next to a river with potentially good campsites. Try to approximate when you'd hit the harder parts of the trail (first thing in the morning on fresh legs? Or at the end of the day after making miles?). Will the trail go above tree line, and can you get through those miles before afternoon thunderstorms hit? How often will you be passing water sources, or will you have to carry water for a long way if the trail is dry? Plot out where your goal camp spots will be each night (and don't forget to check back on this after your trip to see how close you were and adjust for the next trip).

Understand that your first and last days will likely be shorter mileages as you need to account for travel time to and from the destination. Will resupply be needed? If so, how will that be handled? Check the map for nearby towns that may have post offices you could mail a box to or stores you could buy food and supplies from. If the trail doesn't go directly through a town, look for road crossings and figure out if family and friends, a shuttle bus, or a hired car service could be a way to reach civilization, or if someone would be willing to meet you at a trailhead or road crossing to resupply you.

Practice identifying terrain on pretrip day hikes. Take topo maps with you, and every so often work to orient yourself and get a feel for what the topo lines and features translate to in real life. Granted, if you're practicing in one region and traveling to another to backpack, there will be adjustments, but knowing what 1,000 feet of elevation gain in 1 mile versus spread out in 2 miles does to your kids will come in handy when estimating what they are capable of when planning longer trips.

WHEN WILL YOU GO? ASSESSING THE SEASON

Prior to having children, it was easy to take off on a lark without regard to the time of year or weather conditions. Sure, you may get drenched or find yourself post-holing through snow for hours if you're not properly prepared, but at least the only one who ends up miserable is yourself. Once kids are in the picture, it will greatly behoove you to take weather conditions and your progeny's hardiness into account when planning your outing.

Carefully plotting out *when* you will be backpacking is crucial. If your kids are not yet school-age or you homeschool, you have quite a bit of flexibility. Taking trips to popular areas when the majority of folks are bound by school is one of the perks of backpacking with toddlers. If your kids are in school, you might feel limited to weekends and school vacations. Figure out what time of year your trip will be, along with the time of week and even time of day, as all of this will play directly into your plans. Seasons vary widely from place to place, of course, so I'll describe them by their attributes rather than specific months.

Peak Season

Peak season is the ideal time of year to visit an area, and it varies by location. In some regions, like Joshua Tree National Park in California or Big Bend National Park in Texas, peak season is in the winter when temperatures are cool enough to explore their desert landscapes. In Moab, Utah, spring can be a glorious time to explore Canyonlands and Arches National Parks as snow melts on rock formations and the temperatures haven't reached triple digits yet. In the Rocky Mountains of Colorado, late summer is when many eager backpackers have their eyes glued to snowmelt stats every year, waiting for mountain passes in the high country to clear for hiking. Once the snow on the passes melts to a safe level, it is like the hiking gates are opened for the season.

As temperatures get uncomfortably high in some lower elevations, folks like to head for the hills. With wildflower season kicking it off, summer in the mountains can be spectacular. Streams are flowing, which means you don't usually have to carry as much water and you're able to cool off easily and give your kids a fun place to play (more on that in Chapter 7, "Considering Distances"). Birds are chirping, and you may see more animals out and about. Everything is green and vibrant and smells good. I would not blame you one bit if you spin around with your arms open wide, singing about the hills being alive. Many kids are on break, so this is the prime time for parents to go on the epic adventure they've been dreaming of.

If you're planning on backpacking a high-use area during peak season, be sure to research permits and regulations, which I'll talk about more in the next section. Aside from the crowds, another downside of hiking this time of year is that bugs are typically at their peak as well. We'll talk more about those later in the book (see p. 158).

In some mountain regions, afternoon storms can be a daily occurrence during peak season. Plan your trips accordingly and know what to do in case of sudden storms, which is discussed further in Chapter 12, "Overcoming Obstacles." In general, do not enter exposed high areas in inclement weather. If you're on a backpacking trip that requires going over mountain passes, try to time going over the passes early in the day before storms have a chance to build. If you need to get over a pass but clouds are building or a storm rolls in, consider moving to lower ground, setting up your tent, and playing some games while waiting out the storm. Or open your umbrellas and eat. Stay safe and keep up a positive attitude. The kids will be taking their cues from you.

After Peak Season

The typical peak season is followed by a season of cooler temperatures, sometimes below freezing at night, and the potential for early winter weather. Seasonal water sources may have dried up by this time. It may be peak fire season in some areas. One good thing about a reduction of water is that it comes with the reduction of bugs. Also, by this time, many families of school-aged kids are back to the daily grind, leaving popular areas far less populated. Backpacking during this season can be beautiful and somewhat more stable in terms of weather as well. In the high country, above tree line, there are typically fewer thunderstorm/lightning concerns. If you're in a region where trees change colors, it can be stunning.

The days are shorter and colder though, and snow can come early. My first backpacking trip in Colorado was in early October, and we got unexpectedly snowed on. So do your research, try to get some "on-the-ground" intel from the Internet or public land management agencies if possible, and be prepared. For information on water availability and snowpack levels, SNOTEL measurements through the National Water and Climate Center and US Forest Service ranger stations are excellent resources. We have called the offices of the national parks and Forest Service for such information. Hiking apps and websites can also offer user reports on trail conditions, but be aware, conditions change constantly.

Coldest Months of the Year

Options abound for camping during the coldest months of the year. Coastal regions, lower elevations, desert options, and lower latitudes can all provide fun year-round backpacking. Depending on where you are headed, you'll need to adjust your gear based on the expected temperature ranges (heavier sleeping bags or quilts for colder nights). If you are skilled in camping in the snow, consider introducing your kids to that experience as well. Research what overnight temperatures will be and make plans for how to keep your bodies comfortable in those conditions. Keep in mind that the winter months also come with much shorter days. You may end up with many hours in the dark after sunset but before bedtime.

The Thaw

In snowy climates, with the thaw comes the start of mud season. Trails can become one long mud trough that you'll be tempted to skirt around, but don't. Doing so causes erosion to the environment surrounding the path, so stay on the trail, muddy though it may be. Understand that if you go backpacking in this season, you'll likely end up with filthy shoes and pants.

Runoff in streams can be highest as daytime temperatures start to climb, making this season the most dangerous for water crossings (more on that on p. 168). Keep in mind that the runoff reaches peak flows later in the afternoon after the sun has had all day to melt the snow, and then water levels drop overnight as temperatures cool (so, that raging stream will typically be easiest and safest to cross first thing in the morning!). In some places, bugs begin to come out. In the desert and other hot environments, this time is prime for backpacking because seasonal water may still be available and temperatures haven't reached miserable heat levels yet.

Weather Sites

When checking conditions in the backcountry, here are some useful sites, apps, and resources:

▸ NOAA's weather site has good descriptions of when weather systems will hit and of the directions systems are moving *weather.gov*

▸ SNOTEL measurements through the National Water and Climate Center *nrcs.usda.gov*

▸ US Forest Service ranger stations *fs.usda.gov*

▸ Weather Underground *wunderground.com*

▸ Mountain Forecast *mountain-forecast.com*

HOW WILL YOU GO?
PERMITS AND RESERVATIONS

As the number of visitors to the backcountry continues to rise and land managers work to find ways to manage the impact growing crowds have on the backcountry, more areas are moving to a permit or reservation system. Some parks or outdoor areas require a permit to enter. Others have separate or additional permits for particular trails and hikes. There could also be permits or reservations for specific campsites. Permits vary from free, walk-up permits that you fill out at the trailhead to ones that are booked months in advance through various timed-entry reservation systems or lotteries. Today, most popular national parks, such as Yosemite, Yellowstone, Glacier, and Rocky Mountain, require an advance reservation for backcountry campsites. Some will hold a certain percentage of backcountry permits for in-person walk-ups the day of or the day before your trip, but it's not something to count on.

The list of popular backcountry areas that require advance reservations or lotteries is growing every year. The plus side to this shift to advance reservations is that the overall number of people in the backcountry at any one time is kept at a reasonable level, which helps preserve some of the solitude of the wild and reduces impacts. The downside is that it requires a lot of advance planning (and stress if the permits are reserved within minutes of being released), and it reduces the ability to do spontaneous trips on short notice in these places.

Permits: The Lowdown

Figure out which agency manages the area you're interested in backpacking and check out their website, map of the area, or give them a call to determine what type of permit, if any, is required and how to acquire it. The following is a general progression of regulations from least to most restrictive:

▸ **No permits or reservations required.** In this case, you can just show up and start walking.

▸ **Free or low-cost permit.** Sometimes a permit is required but it is free or low cost. These tend to be available to pick up on the day of your hike at a government office or at the trailhead.

▸ **Walk-up permit.** At some popular spots, a percentage of available permits are held for walk-up reservations. Be sure to find out what time the permit desk opens as a line can form early in the morning for these coveted permits.

▸ **Location-specific permit.** Many desirable locations require advance reservations for a particular camping zone (Grand Tetons for example), trailhead entry (Yosemite), or specific campsite (Rocky Mountain National Park).

▸ **Lottery system permit.** In recent years, some heavily traveled spots have begun to offer advance reservations that are available via a lottery system only. Oftentimes there is a nonrefundable fee to enter the lottery.

When you begin researching areas for a backpacking trip, spend time assessing an area's current requirements, as these may make or break your ultimate decision to backpack there. Note that the permit and reservation systems can (and frequently do!) change, so it's a good idea to research even the areas you've been to in the past to see if there are new entry requirements or regulations.

Reserving a Campsite

Reservable campsites tend to be in heavily traveled areas or areas that are environmentally sensitive. Most of the popular national parks (for example, Rocky Mountain, Glacier, Grand Tetons, Yellowstone, Yosemite) require advance reservations for backcountry sites. Some places with mostly reservable sites will hold a few permits aside for walk-up backpackers, but you'll need to be flexible on where you're going—a challenging situation with kids along.

The land management agency will have information on their website on how to reserve sites. In popular areas, they may open for reservations four to six months (or more) ahead of time and may get booked out quickly. It is always a good idea to check what their process is and familiarize yourself with their popularity and permitting season. If you can't find the information online, I have found it useful to call their office directly and ask how quickly sites book up.

Plan your route, estimated mileage for each day, and roughly where you'd like to end up with the available campsites or zones

Kaleo, Malia, and Rae in Colorado's Flat Tops Wilderness during mosquito season. Photo by David Heinrich

in mind. Have a backup site or plan ready as well, in case there is a frenzy on the morning sites open up and you don't get your first choice. This happened to us when we were booking a backpacking trip in Banff, Canada. All the campsites for the entire summer opened up on a single morning, and the website continually crashed. By the time we got through, our first choices were completely booked, and we quickly had to figure out a plan B (and C).

Backcountry permits are often free or low cost, but some highly trafficked areas can have higher fees (see "Permits: The Lowdown" for a breakdown of permit types, p. 16). There are two different specificity levels of the reservation system.

1. **Designated campsite.** This is the most rigid site selection, where you reserve a specific campsite for the night. The pros are that you know you have a place to sleep and don't need to worry about finding something suitable. The cons are that if your mileage ends up changing, you can find yourself struggling to make it to the site or having to end your day early if you get to the site ahead of schedule. This can come into play on longer, multiday trips, especially when you're not yet familiar with your family's typical daily mileage/pace. It can also be tricky when booking multiday trips if sites that you planned on reserving are not available on your designated day.

2. **Designated zones.** Sometimes you reserve a spot in a camping zone, not a particular site, for example along the Teton Crest Trail in Grand Teton National Park, Wyoming. Zones vary in size and are marked on the trail with start and end posts. Within the zone, there are various sites, and you hike until you find an available spot that suits your particular needs. In the Indian Peaks Wilderness in Colorado, a permit is necessary to camp in the various zones, but there are no specific sites within the zones. Designated zone permits offer the most flexible amount of travel in reservable areas. Furthermore, the regulatory agencies ensure that the areas aren't overused by limiting the number of permits issued.

Nonreservable Sites

Nonreservable, first-come-first-served, or dispersed sites offer the freedom of flexibility and ease of planning. Wilderness areas, state parks, BLM, and Forest Service land can provide an opportunity to get out on a backpacking trip without any reservations. Be sure to research the area you're interested in to understand what the regulations are. If you're not sure how far your kids will be able to hike in a day, these areas are incredibly forgiving because you can set up camp wherever the terrain allows regardless of how far in you've walked.

Be aware that areas that may have once been first-come-first-served or did not require a permit in the past may not be the same now. As backpacking popularity has grown, some places have instituted a permit process to manage the impact on popular areas. Also be aware that most dispersed sites don't have facilities, meaning no bathrooms or picnic tables.

The bottom line is to do research ahead of time and know what your risk tolerance is. Have a backup plan if you don't have

PRO TIP

DID YOU KNOW that wilderness areas have the highest level of protection of all federal lands? No logging, mining, or roads are allowed. These areas offer some of the most pristine (and scenic) landscapes and generally don't require advance reservations. This makes them ideal for planning your next backpacking adventure.

a reservation. Use the winter months with longer nights to start your summer backpacking planning. Once you know when and where you are going, be sure to send copies of your itineraries to a few different people, along with expected check-in times and days.

2

Food Planning

FIGURING OUT WHAT FOOD and how much of it you need to pack may be one of the hardest parts of backpacking when you are taking kids with you. Kids' consumption varies so much from year to year (even day to day), and preferences change. It is hard enough to prepare a dinner everyone will eat at home, let alone in the middle of the woods where pickings are slim and there are no other options.

Planning is crucial, and you shouldn't assume that what worked the last time your family backpacked will work this time. Therefore, every time you take a backpacking trip, you need to recalculate how much food your kids will eat on the trail. They will likely eat more than they did the previous summer. How much more, however, is at best an educated guess.

Always be sure to pack more and play the "better safe than sorry" game. Bring an extra dinner, extra snacks, and calculate your pace conservatively, underestimating how many miles your kids will be able to hike in a day. By being cautious, we have only come close to running out of food once. Or maybe twice. But we never actually ran out, and the kids never went hungry.

In this section, we look at meal planning and how to predict how much you should bring, as well as at some backpacking-friendly foods and tips on meal prep you can do prior to hitting the trail.

MEAL PLANNING

A full day on the trail will typically include breakfast, four snacks, and dinner. In our family, we've done away with the lunch idea because we find ourselves grazing at many of our breaks. Dinner is often cooked at a water source, so some days we end up having dinner in the middle of the day if we know that will be our only water source for the day.

Once you know how many days you will be out on the trail, you can figure out how many meals you need. Each of these meals feeds your whole family, so each dinner is planned to be large enough for everyone; same with snacks (for sake of easy calculations). For example, if you're starting your hike on a Friday afternoon and will be back by Sunday afternoon, you might need two dinners (Friday and Saturday), two breakfasts (Saturday and Sunday), and nine or ten snacks, depending on timing.

The caloric size of each of those meals depends on family size and needs. A pair of adults hiking with a single toddler will require much less food than a family of adults and multiple

Malia and Rae during a shoes-off snack break on the Colorado Trail.
Photo by David Heinrich

teens. Keeping in mind that on some breaks, we don't eat much, and on other breaks we eat a ton, it all evens out. Also, we tend to bring along a few extra snacks. An easy extra go-to snack is a nut-heavy trail mix because it is calorically dense. On longer hikes, we always bring an extra dinner or two, as well, if we aren't exactly sure how hungry we'll be and as a safety measure if we end up spending an extra night out there.

If you're heading out late in the day on Friday, a fun treat (that also makes the first night's dinner a snap) is to buy deli sandwiches, burritos, or some other easy to-go meal that doesn't have much waste or require utensils. You can carry this premade meal in your packs to the spot where you'll stop for dinner. On one of our longer hikes, we'd stopped at a pizza restaurant near the trail for dinner. When we couldn't finish all the food, we asked for it to be wrapped in foil, which allowed us to fit it in our bear bag. Waking up the next morning and having delicious—albeit cold—pizza instead of the regular breakfast shake was a treat that the kids remember to this day.

On shorter trips—such as a one-nighter to test out how things go—keep meals simple and fun so the kids have great memories of their time in the woods. Don't be afraid to substitute king-size candy bars for sports bar alternatives. They are cheaper and pack just as much caloric punch (sometimes more) as your typical energy bar. Be aware, however, that milk chocolate melts quite easily in warmer temperatures. Dark chocolate is more durable.

For trips where temperatures will be high, consider bringing a larger quantity of salty foods to replace the sodium that your bodies are sure to lose through sweat. Many nut-based trail mixes, chips, and pretzels are perfect for this.

Don't forget about fresh fruits and vegetables. Many do not need refrigeration and can be taken in the backcountry. Particularly hearty (less likely to wilt or bruise) fruits include apples, oranges, and grapes. Carrots, onions, cherry tomatoes, potatoes, avocados, spinach, broccoli, cauliflower, peppers, and cucumber can all go for days without refrigeration. Harder cheeses, like cheddar, parmesan, and aged mozzarella, can often go a few days without refrigeration too if the temperature is mild. These may not be the foods you gravitate to for a quick weekend trip, as these foods are heavier and may create waste of peels or cores, but if you're on a longer multiweek backpacking trip, the taste and freshness will be well worth it at resupply points. Our kids love juicy apple slices out on the trail. A Swiss Army knife can be used to easily share one fruit between all of us. When we backpack with our dog, we feed the core to her after removing the seeds (otherwise we'd pack it out).

Dehydrated Meals and Snacks

Dehydrated meals are available at most outdoor stores and online and can offer a variety of meals for easy planning. They get expensive pretty quickly though. If this is something you think you'll be doing frequently, consider buying a dehydrator.

Food dehydrators are a great investment if you're going to be doing a lot of trips. You can make a variety of foods for the trail and to more easily pack meals in advance. They allow you to know exactly what goes into your food and will cut food costs in the long run.

Dave bought me a dehydrator for my birthday a few years ago, and our homemade dried mango is better than anything you can buy at the store. We've experimented with dehydrating smoothies, chilis, hummus, pickles, fruits, veggies, beans, tofu, all sorts of things. Google is your friend—check out different blogs and articles for ideas. There are also a number of great books out there for making your own dehydrated food.

Experimenting with a dehydrator can be a fun way to get the kids involved, too. Letting them choose snacks and meals helps get their buy-in and hopefully gets them excited for the upcoming trip. As a note, be aware that if there are fats in the meal that you dehydrate, the meal will need to be refrigerated, as it will become rancid after a while. Research how to safely store dehydrated foods, and consider investing in a vacuum sealer.

Dehydrated snacks can be one key piece of the backpacking food puzzle. What other foods are good to take on a trip? Dried fruit, nuts, bars, chips, crackers, cookies, and tortillas with peanut butter are all excellent options with decent calorie-to-ounce ratios. Things that don't pack very well are breads, soft fruits (bananas, pears, and peaches), canned foods (heavy), anything in a glass container, and individually wrapped foods that create a lot of small garbage that can blow away easily.

Calories and Pack Weight

When considering food options, remember that the lighter it is, the easier to carry, so the weight-to-nutritional-value ratio (how many calories per ounce of weight) should factor into what you choose to bring along. Pure olive oil is 250 calories per ounce, an apple is 15 calories per ounce, and a snickers bar is 139 calories per ounce, for comparison. Thus, sometimes you may need to opt for foods that are perhaps less beloved by your kids but that pack a serious energy punch for their weight. You can explain to your kids, if they are old enough, that taste, variety, simplicity, and durability are important when backpacking.

The FDA recommends 2,000 calories per adult per day as a general guide for nutrition at home. However, Andrew Skurka, seasoned backpacker and outdoor guide, suggests on his website 3,000 calories per adult per day when backpacking. We divide our daily caloric goal up to get about 20 percent of those calories at dinner, 20 percent at breakfast, and the rest as snacks at 15 percent each four times a day. This is a rough guide for planning purposes only. Adjust to meet your family's unique dietary needs. Take a look at what each person in your family eats in a day at home and bump it up to account for increased appetites while hiking.

When our kids were toddlers and we weren't hiking far, we'd stay close to our normal 2,000 calories per day each for my husband and I, with 1,000 to 2,000 calories for each of the kids. These trips were so short that even if they ate more than we expected, we'd be covered with the extra snack bag of trail mix that we always brought along.

All that said, you absolutely don't need to count calories! Some people eyeball it; some people approximate weight. (Andrew Skurka suggests 1.5 to 2 pounds of food per adult per day.) Do what works for you and adjust for the next trip as needed.

Pretrip Meal Assembling

Once you know how many breakfasts, snacks, and dinners you need for the trip, you can begin to assemble some of those meals in advance. Zip-top plastic bags are your friends here. They are resealable, waterproof, and allow you to easily see the contents.

In our house, every person's breakfast gets its own bag. Every snack gets its own bag. When the food in the bag is eaten,

Our food for 80 miles of the Tahoe Rim Trail with a partial resupply 42 miles in. Some dinners aren't shown.

the bag can be reused as a toilet paper bag or a garbage bag or packed out to be reused on another trip.

We cook all our dinners in one pot, so when we are prepping the food prior to the trip, we combine all the ingredients for a dinner into one larger zip-top plastic bag, including smaller sealable bags within the larger bag that contain spices or cheese that are added at different points in the cooking process.

Some ingredients may need to stay refrigerated until your trip (be sure not to forget them!). If a dinner has special preparation notes, write these on a piece of paper and include it in the bag. Once you're organized, begin assembling by laying the bags out on the floor so you can see how many of each meal category you have.

Snacks such as crackers, chips, pretzels, and trail mix get repackaged into bags. We aim to have each bag contain some multiple of a snack (roughly 1,000 calories for our family). For example, a quart-size bag of crackers might be one snack, but a quart of nuts might be two-plus snacks. For planning and easy reference on the trail, use a permanent marker to write your

---

PRO TIP

WHEN IT COMES TO SHARING FOOD, it is good practice to use hand sanitizer before digging into communal bags, when possible. Alternatively, you can shake food out into waiting, cupped hands or have separate bags for each person.

A Day on the Trail: Sample Meal Plan

BREAKFAST   Packet of Carnation Breakfast powder mixed with ground instant oats. Dump mix into a half-full water bottle, shake it up, and drink it down.

SNACKS/LUNCH   Rolled tortilla with peanut butter and Nutella, crackers with avocado, trail mix, energy bars.

DINNER   Prepackaged blend of ramen mixed with a cup of instant brown rice (and dehydrated veggies, if desired). Empty into a pot of boiling water, add some oil. Eat directly from pot. Simple to make, and the salts from the flavor-packet paired with warm noodles make a tasty, comforting end-of-day meal.

estimate of how many snacks it counts as on the frosted label on the front of each bag so you can easily add them all up.

Store-bought bars don't get repackaged. Most fresh fruits and veggies don't get repackaged either. We also don't usually count fresh fruits or veggies toward our daily calorie requirements because they don't have many calories at all, but they are loaded with vitamins, and we end up craving the juicy crunch of apples, carrots, and other raw produce when we are out on the trail eating lots of salty prepared stuff all day.

PART 2

PREP

3

Packs, Sleeps, and Shelter

THIS IS THE CHUNKIEST SECTION in the book, with good reason! I want you to be prepared out there, which means discussing all the gear. You've done the planning—you know how long you'll be on the trail, the general climate and terrain you'll encounter, and as the date approaches, what sort of weather systems you might expect. You've planned the meals, dehydrating and prepping some of your food in advance. Now, use all that information to determine the gear you'll be taking with you.

The abundance of options for backpacking gear is mind-boggling. A quick online search will result in copious lists and charts outlining the latest and greatest items to improve your adventure. Don't feel overwhelmed by all of that. I assure you, you can keep it simple, choosing gear that keeps you comfortable while not breaking the bank or your back.

To help you sort it all out, Part 2 covers the essential backpacking gear. This includes the Big Three: (backpack, sleeping system, shelter); clothing; footwear; and other key gear, such as cooking systems and water purification.

Remember as you read through Part 2 that the marketplace for backpacking gear is constantly expanding and evolving. Cottage manufacturers and big-box retailers are excited to tout the groundbreaking tweaks made to designs and materials, but keep in mind that it isn't always necessary to have the most cutting-edge or priciest items. This section will explain what to look for in various pieces of gear. What you absolutely need—and what you can live without.

Let's start by taking a look at the Big Three!

BACKPACKS

While backpacks are the first Big Three gear item that we'll discuss, I suggest that you make this purchase last, once you figure out the rest of the gear. If you've never owned a backpacking pack before, I recommend going to an outdoor store to try on various packs in person. Walk around the store and grab mock-up gear of what you'll be putting in your pack, and see how it all fits in the different capacity bags. This will help you determine how large of a pack you'll need for your gear. Work to narrow your packing list as much as possible before choosing a pack. Fewer things to carry means a smaller and lighter-weight pack, which reduces your overall carrying weight.

Many packs, especially those found at the big-box stores, are reinforced and overly stout in order to boost their durability, but this adds ounces and even pounds to the design. Many pack makers are more worried about unnecessary returns than your overall pack weight. There is also the assumption that you're carrying traditional (heavy) loads and need frames designed to distribute the weight to help manage it all. Try looking at some of the online cottage retailers that are making packs out of sturdy but lighter-weight fabrics. Once you have an idea of how much space you need to fit your gear, you'll have a better idea of how that translates when looking at packs online that you can't touch in person. Some shops also offer robust customer service via phone or email that will answer all sorts of questions you might have, helping you find a pack that best fits your needs.

Backpack Weight

Since this book is geared toward backpacking with children, let's take a closer look at what kids, specifically, can carry. When backpacking with kids even as young as age 2, have them carry some gear. At first, keep it minimal just to have them get used to the idea. Young children love mimicking adults (how many want to play with our phones?) and will get a kick out of carrying their own small pack for a short amount of time.

As for what they'll bring, when your kids are young, let them pack some things that they want. A few race cars, some little dinosaurs or dolls, maybe a couple of small books or crayons and paper. A light, plastic magnifying glass can be fun for examining flowers and bugs, as can a light pair of binoculars. A yummy snack treat. Water. Make sure whatever they bring is easy to clean and is not going to devastate them if destroyed, lost, or dropped in a creek.

But how much should a child carry? Expert opinions vary slightly, but all agree that the pack should be under 20 percent of body weight. On the conservative side, medical experts at the American Occupational Therapy Association have recommended that kids limit what they carry to 10 percent of their body weight. Meanwhile, Dr. Pierre d'Hemecourt with the Sports Medicine Division at Boston Children's Hospital has advised that an adolescent could carry from 15 percent to a maximum of 20 percent of body weight, depending on fitness and growth period. Sutter Health, a nonprofit medical center in Northern California, concurs, advising that a full backpack should weigh between 10 to 20 percent of a child's body weight. And in a 2019 article for Backpacker.com titled "How Far Can Kids Hike, and How Much Can They Carry?" Dr. Stephanie Canale and Tod Schimelpfenig (curriculum director for National Outdoor Leadership School Wilderness Medicine) suggest kids younger than 7 limit it to 5 to 10 percent, and for older kids to err toward 15 percent rather than pushing to 20 percent. Given all that, we try to stick to the 10 to 15 percent guideline where possible.

Using the rough guidelines of a pack being 10 to 20 percent of a child's body weight, I created the chart on the next page.

When we first started backpacking with our kids over a decade ago, there weren't many lightweight options in kids' packs. Traditional kids' backpacks can weigh over three pounds empty! A pack that is already three or more pounds wouldn't

Rough Guide to Pack Weight

WEIGHT OF CHILD	MAX WEIGHT OF PACK (10%–20%)
30 lbs.	3–6 lbs.
50 lbs.	5–10 lbs.
80 lbs.	8–16 lbs.
100 lbs.	10–20 lbs.

be able to add much gear before reaching the weight limits of what a kid should carry. Today more companies offer kid-specific lines.

It is fine to get your kid started in an affordable pack from a big-box store when they are young enough to not need frames. Once they start carrying their own sleeping bag and need more capacity, it is prudent to explore your options, including the lightweight ones.

Style and Fit

In our family, we all tend to prefer rucksack-style packs, with one large interior storage area and a large, mesh pocket on the front for quick-access items. Side pockets for water bottles, poles, and umbrellas are great. Some also come with an internal hydration sleeve pocket for water bladders. A small interior zip pocket is great for keys, phones, or small, special toys. A couple exterior straps or loops can be handy to fasten camp shoes or wet items, but whenever possible, store items within the pack rather than hanging things off it.

Fit is very important. The pack should be snug to the back with straps at 90-degree angles to the shoulders (not below or above). Hip belts (if there are any) should cinch around the hips, not the waist.

At first, the size and weight of their packs will dictate what kids are able to carry. When our kids were between 2 and 5 years old, they'd carry their own child-size hydration packs, which held 1.5 liters of water and left a little space for gear. A couple of bars, some trinkets, a beanie, warm gloves, and maybe a light jacket filled that space.

As kids get older, they'll be able to carry more of their own gear. When my son was 4, he graduated to an 18-liter capacity youth pack as he wasn't carrying his sleeping bag yet. It was big enough to carry his sleeping pad and all his clothes.

We tried a few different packs of varying weights and capacities for my daughter. One pack she tried ended up digging into her shoulders the first day of hiking; another didn't have the capacity that she needed for both her sleeping bag and warm

PRO TIP

THERE IS A LOT OF TRIAL AND ERROR in finding the perfect pack, so be sure to check return policies for all gear that you purchase. Once you find a pack that works, don't be afraid to make modifications to it, cutting off straps or parts that your child won't use in order to lighten the load and improve usability or comfort.

Kaleo (7) and Rae (9) with homemade backpacks (Teton Crest Trail, Wyoming).

coat. Luckily, we were able to return both, and I ended up sewing her one using Jardine's Ray-Way kit (see the "Helpful Resources" section for website).

When they got even older (around age 7), they carried a slightly larger pack to accommodate the sleeping bag.

By age 10 or 11, our kids were over five feet tall. Following the manufacturers' sizing charts, we found extra-small packs that were technically made for adults and comfortably held everything they needed, plus some food. The main drawback on the packs I'd sewn was they didn't have hip-belt pockets to hold snacks and cameras. These adult packs did, while remaining

What Should My Child Carry?

For kids under age 4, start them off on the right foot by keeping their pack really light and letting them select what they want to bring. They could start with a small hydration or other low-capacity pack.

UNDER AGE 4

- ☐ Toys
- ☐ A favorite treat
- ☐ Water (start with a very small amount and gradually increase). Use a wide-mouth water bottle if they don't use the hydration pack.

FROM AGES 4 TO 7

They might be responsible for everything above, plus:

- ☐ Sleeping pad
- ☐ Mosquito head net
- ☐ Umbrella
- ☐ Water
- ☐ Stuffed animal/toy of choice
- ☐ Whistle
- ☐ Headlamp
- ☐ Sun hat
- ☐ Sunglasses
- ☐ Bandanna

- ☐ Extra clothes:
  1 shirt, 2 pairs socks, 2 pairs underwear, 2 pants or shorts (or one of each), long underwear top and bottom for sleep/warmth, wind jacket, warm jacket, warm hat, mittens/gloves, neck gaiter/scarf, camp shoes

FROM AGES 7 TO EARLY TEEN

They might be responsible for everything from ages 4 to 7, plus:

☐ Sleeping bag

FROM MID- TO OLDER TEEN

They might be responsible for everything listed above plus:

☐ Tent or part of the tent

☐ Cook stuff

☐ Food

☐ Anything adults carry (they may take their own backpacking trips, or trips with Scouts or other groups, and will be in charge of carrying their own system, which would include all the additional kits, like fire-starter kit, first aid kit, toiletries kit, water purification system, etc.)

lightweight. We still carried the second tent for the kids (at this point, they slept in one two-person tent, and Dave and I slept in another), though it did fit in that pack.

As your children mature, you can decide if you'd like to save a little bit of weight by having them carry only one extra pair of shorts or pants, socks, and underwear. At some point, their desire for privacy or interest in camping with people other than your family may lead to them carrying their own tent. Celebrate the milestone while continuing to keep an eye on their pack weight.

SLEEP SYSTEMS

After a long day of walking, climbing into your tent and getting cozy in your sleep system can be blissful. The second item of the Big Three gear pieces, the sleep system, is whatever you sleep under or inside of at night (shelter systems, such as tents, will be discussed later in this chapter). Major decisions in this category are temperature rating, down versus synthetic fill, and sleeping bag versus quilt.

Temperature Rating

The sleep system you're looking at, whether it is a bag or a quilt, should have a temperature rating on it. Bags can range from below freezing on up, with colder temperature ratings typically being more expensive. Keep in mind that these ratings may feel different from brand to brand (and from person to person!). Some companies approach the rating with a "this will keep you alive down to this point" mindset, while others approach it with a "this will keep you comfortable down to this point" approach. There is a massive difference between comfortable and alive!

The temperature rating you choose depends on where and what time of year you'll be camping, but it is also about personal preference. I tend to get cold at night, so I like a bag with a lower temperature rating than what the actual temperature might be. My husband sleeps warmer, however, and can be comfortable in a bag with a 10-to-15 degree higher rating than mine.

Our kids have always been fairly warm sleepers. When they were infants and we car camped, we'd dress them in layers because we couldn't use blankets. It was like swaddling to the max. Because of this, we didn't do much backpacking till they were a bit better at regulating body temperature by burrowing deeper into sleeping bags or unzipping them. We only backpacked when we knew the night temperatures were mild enough that no actual harm would come to them if they were exposed to the elements or not on their sleep pad all night. If you are a co-sleeping family, look for sleeping bags that can zip together or larger quilt options so you can all share each other's body heat.

The Filling

Down is animal (goose or duck) plumage—the soft, wispy stuff under the exterior feathers. It is very lightweight and compactable, lending itself well to backpacking trips where space and weight are at a premium. Down also tends to last longer than synthetic fibers. A high-quality down bag can last a decade or more when properly cared for.

The downside to down is moisture. Down loses much of its insulative value when it gets wet, and it does not dry quickly, so it is imperative to keep down away from water. Because its insulation comes from the loft (air space) between feathers, no loft means no warmth. The loft can be significantly compromised when wet.

Wet down also has the tendency to clump, which can lead to cold spots if the down is not evenly redistributed. We often pull our down sleeping bags/quilts out of the tent in the morning to dry a bit in the sun if possible. A sunny break spot is also a great way to dry any damp items.

Down can be particularly problematic if camping in humid areas as it tends to build up moisture with continued use. Finally, cleaning down sleeping bags requires special detergents suitable for down, and it can take many hours in a dryer (with tennis balls deployed for declumping) to get them dry.

Synthetic fill is man-made fiber, typically polyester. While more affordable than down, unfortunately, it is also generally heavier and less compactable than down. The good news is that it continues to insulate when wet. And when it is dirty, you can simply stick it in the washing machine with regular detergent and hang it outside to dry. This easy-to-wash feature made it our go-to bag when our kids were young (see "Potty Training and Sleep Systems" on p. 49).

Sleeping Bag versus Quilt

Sleeping bags are quite literally bags that you sleep in. They typically have a zipper on one side, wrap fully around your body, enclose your feet, and can have a hood with a drawstring that goes over your head. Backpacking sleeping bags are often mummy shaped, tapering down from widest at the shoulders to narrowest at the feet to reduce the air volume that your body needs to heat within the bag.

Quilts are like backpacking blankets. You can find them at cottage manufacturers or other backpacking-gear outlets. I recommend checking online to see if the store of your choice car-

Rae (8) and I drinking breakfast shakes while airing out our quilt (yellow and black) and the kids' sleeping bags. It is good to air them out daily on a long trip as the body gives off moisture throughout the night that gets trapped in the down (Tahoe Rim Trail, Nevada). Photo by David Heinrich

ries them. If you are handy with a sewing machine, you can also make them yourself using patterns. Search for "down backpacking quilt pattern," and a number of options will pop up. I used the down quilt kit and instructions from Thru-hiker.com for the quilt Dave and I have been using since 2006.

Many quilts have a footbox sewn at the bottom to stick your feet into. The majority of the quilt drapes over your body, and you are able to tuck it under yourself with some extra material on the sides. Some are part of systems that attach to sleep pads to prevent drafts using a strap, and others offer a snap at the neck to minimize drafts.

One advantage of quilts is that they do not have zippers, which reduces their weight. Another reason that backpackers choose quilts over sleeping bags is that the part of the sleeping bag that is underneath you gets compressed and doesn't really add to your warmth. Eliminating this bottom portion as well as a zipper lowers not just the weight but also the size of the gear (a major focus in backpacking lighter).

Then there's the comfort factor. For folks who move around in their sleep (which kids tend to do a lot of) or who aren't back sleepers, a quilt can be more comfortable than a mummy bag as it is more similar to your home sleeping arrangement. For kids newer to camping, it is an easy transition to being covered in a bed by blankets to being covered by a quilt. If you find your child has a hard time keeping it on, there are strap options that wrap the sides of the quilt securely under the sleeping pad.

Finally, the ability to regulate temperature by sticking a knee or leg out from under a quilt on warm evenings is a definite perk. This prevents your body from overheating and sweating, which leads to reduced moisture in the quilt.

If you sleep with a partner, you can get a two-person quilt and save additional weight and space. A disadvantage of a two-person quilt is that it can get quite drafty around the shoulder and neck areas if your partner is a side sleeper and you are not. My personal solution is to pack my down jacket between our shoulders or even wear it on really cold nights until I warm up.

Quilts have become more mainstream since we used ours on our PCT hike in 2006, and I would recommend them to anyone looking for equipment for themselves or for their children. It can take a bit of practice to get used to sleeping with them, so take some shorter trips in moderate temperatures to get the hang of it. There are a number of quilt companies that make single or dual quilts and even youth quilts (see the "Helpful Resources" section).

Potting Training and Sleep Systems

Since this is a book about backpacking with kids, I'd be remiss if I didn't address the issue of potty training. It has its challenges, but don't let that stop you from taking your kids on overnight trips in their early years.

On our first few backpacking trips, our children weren't fully potty trained, and we dealt with some wet nights. On our very first trip, in fact, one of the kids woke up wet, we got them changed, and then they slept on me for the rest of the night. (The next morning, I informed my husband we were cutting our trip short, and we headed home that day.)

Sometimes they'd sleep through it, and we'd deal with cleanup in the morning. If the bag isn't soaked all the way through, you can turn it inside out and put a blanket inside against the nylon to make it more comfortable. If they won't get back in their bag, they can always squeeze into your bag with you if they're small, or you can unzip your bag and use it as a blanket over both of you.

The next morning, put the sleeping bag out in the sun so it can dry as much as possible and be used again the next night. Of course, when you get home, the bags (and children) get a good washing.

Potty training should be a consideration when weighing whether to go with a down or synthetic-filled sleeping system. Synthetic is best until you are fairly certain that your kids will be dry through the night. And just because they've been dry at home for a while doesn't mean they'll be able to stay that way after a day of physically exhausting exertion. It is far easier to throw a synthetic bag or quilt into the washing machine once you're home than it is to clean a down one.

While washable, quick-drying synthetic bags are a wise choice for kids in potty training, unfortunately, they don't compress into a backpack as easily as down, so my husband often ended up strapping them to the exterior of his external frame pack. Once we were pretty confident the kids were potty trained and could start going farther distances, we gave them our old down sleeping bags. They were way too big for them to begin with, but they've grown into them well and will continue to be able to use them for years.

If you are concerned that extra space inside the bag is causing your kids to be cold at night, you can tie a length of paracord around the bag a few inches below their feet or tuck the extra sleeping bag back under their legs so they only have to heat up the air in the bag space that they are using.

If you don't have hand-me-down or inexpensive down mummy bags to give them, consider quilts, as they may be a great option.

Sleeping Pads

Sleeping pads are what you put your sleeping bag or quilt on. Sleep pads provide a welcome buffer of insulation between the floor of your tent (or the earth, or the ground cloth) and your body.

An important factor when selecting a sleep pad is the R-value, which is a measure of the insulating value. The higher the R-value, the better the pad is at dealing with colder ground temperatures. R-values for sleeping pads range from 1 to 5+. Anything over 5 is great for extreme cold camping.

The two main types of sleeping pads are solid pads (closed-cell or eggcrate foam) and inflatable pads. Let's take a look at each and discuss their pros and cons.

Closed-Cell/Eggcrate Foam Pad (R-Value = 2). If you are in the market for new pads and will be doing primarily warm-weather camping, I recommend looking at the closed-cell, eggcrate-looking pads. They tend to be durable and easy to set up by simply unfolding, and they make great seats during rest breaks.

These can be a great choice for kids because of their durability. Our constantly moving kids rarely spend a whole night on their pads anyway, so having something that can handle their beatings is a great idea! The pad's rigidity can also provide you with a "frame" feeling in your backpack when using a lightweight rucksack-style backpack. Simply fold it in nicely against the back interior of your pack. And if you're interested in saving weight (of course you are!), you can cut them down to whatever size you want.

We used this type of pad for the first 1,300 miles of our PCT thru-hike, when we were trying to be *ultra*-ultralight. I admit, we wound up buying inflatable pads (that our kids are now using) when I decided I needed a bit more cushion.

Inflatable Pads (R-Value = 3+). Inflatable pads come in a variety of sizes, thicknesses, and models. Some are relatively thin and can self-inflate. Some are thicker and offer a substantial cushion and R-value for sleeping. Some can actually zip onto your sleeping bag. Check out women's or short and size-small pads as options if you're trying to cut down on weight. There are also two-person pads if you plan on camping with a partner (but note that these pads aren't huge, so make sure you're comfortable being *very* close to your partner).

Inflatable pads are generally more comfortable than closed-cell pads and provide a greater thermal barrier from the cold ground. By far the biggest downside is that they are prone to punctures, which will result in you slowly starting to feel the ground as you sink lower and lower. As one hiker jokingly told us, inflatable pads are great if you want to sleep on the ground, but not right away.

The setup time and effort are nothing to scoff at either. As the designated inflator for our family of four, I can tell you that I have become light-headed on a few occasions.

Avid backpacker, blogger, and author of *How to Survive Your First Trip in the Wild*, Paul "Mags" Magnanti suggests a back-packing hack of using a very thin (one-eighth inch) foam pad to place on the bottom of the expensive, more delicate inflatable pad. The foam is light and inexpensive, and as a bonus, you can use it as a sit pad on breaks or in camp.

Regardless of what kind of pad you choose, you may find that your kids slide off it during the night. Solutions for sliding off pads include getting a nonslip cover for your pad or putting the pad inside the sleeping bag with them.

Sleeping Pads: Pros and Cons

CLOSED-CELL PADS

Lightweight, durable,
quick setup, affordable,
can't puncture,
can be used as a seat
during breaks and as a
"frame" for frameless packs.

Lower R-value, not as
comfortable, can take up
more pack space.

INFLATABLE PADS

Higher R-value,
more comfortable.

Heavier, easily punctured
(need to carry repair kit),
longer setup time,
more expensive,
can't act as a pack frame,
not to be used
as a seat on breaks.

Repairing an Inflatable Pad

If you go to sleep on a cushy, inflated pad only to wake up on the cold, hard ground, it is likely that your pad has a hole in it. Or maybe you didn't close the valve all the way. Blow it up again and see what happens. If you squeeze or lie on the pad, do you hear air escaping? Can you locate the hole? If so, get out your patch kit (that you *always* bring with you) and repair it per the instructions. If you cannot locate the hole, find a large body of water. (Your bathtub works well if you're able to wait until you get home.) The body of water should be fairly still and calm. Inflate your pad, and slowly submerge sections of it. Look for any air bubbles that continuously come from a single point (or multiple points if you're like us and accidentally set up your pad on a cactus).

The source of the air bubbles is the air leaking from your pad. It may take a while to find them. Take your time and thoroughly check all areas of your pad, as there may be multiple holes that you need to patch. If possible, mark each hole with an X over the center of it. Dry the pad thoroughly before attempting to attach a patch to it.

Dave looking for holes in our sleeping pad in a lake in Yellowstone, Wyoming, a minute before finding leeches on his legs.

Pro tip: Watch out for leeches!

SHELTER

The last of the Big Three items to discuss is the backpacking shelter. Shelters on the trail can take many forms. Tents are popular, of course. But some people enjoy camping in hammocks strung between two trees or sleeping under the stars with no shelter at all other than a sleeping bag or quilt. There are also bivy sacks and tarps for the lightest, most minimalist setups.

Our family uses tents. I've cowboy-camped under the stars a time or two on the PCT, and it just isn't for me. I like the privacy and protection (real and perceived) that a thin layer of nylon provides. We camp in places that are fairly buggy, and I prefer that level of separation (from the bugs) while I sleep. If you decide to use a tent, here are some factors to consider when deciding what to buy.

Freestanding versus Nonfreestanding. Nonfreestanding tents use cords that extend to metal stakes driven into the ground to stay upright. If you're camping in very rocky areas, you may need to get creative on how to secure the tie-downs. Freestanding tents hold their form with poles inserted into sleeves and are generally heavier than nonfreestanding tents. With enough gear inside, they may not even need to be staked to the ground. They are great for areas where there are a lot of rocks hidden just below the surface, making staking challenging.

You'll want to consider what kind of surface you'll be setting up camp on. Will the ground be soft enough to drive stakes into? Also consider the weight of each option—although poles make things heavier, know that some tents can utilize trekking poles as substitutes for some or all tent poles, which offers additional weight savings.

Durability. When backpacking with toddlers and very young children, the tent will act as a playpen for the kids, so expect it to need to endure some harsher wear and tear. A helpful way to get an idea of the quality is to read reviews for various tents and brands from several sources. Don't forget to check out YouTube as one potential source of vloggers reviewing products.

Footprint. Consider the size of the tent and how easy or hard it will be to find a place to set it up. Even a standard four-person tent can be tricky to fit within established tent pads. Decide whether your whole family will sleep in one large shelter or if it makes sense to split up into multiple smaller shelters. In the backcountry where tent pads aren't available, it can be easier to find several small, flat clearings to set up multiple tents as opposed to one large one. Depending on your family dynamic, adults can split up and sleep one per shelter with a child until everyone is comfortable with the kids having their own tent. Our kids were 8 and 5 when they shared a "no-adults-allowed" tent the first time. They were 15 and 12 when they decided that, as brother and sister, they wanted their own separate tents.

Single Wall or Double Wall. A single-wall tent, such as a tarp tent, has just a single wall of material to keep the rain out. Mesh will oftentimes be incorporated into the entry, foot, and possibly around the bottom perimeter of the tent to help with ventilation. A double-wall tent often has an inner wall of mostly mesh to help with ventilation and a second wall, or "rainfly," that can be put up when rain is possible. The rainfly of a double-wall tent can work better with more frequent rainstorms as it keeps a barrier between the wet fly and the inside of the tent. On the flip side, having the extra step to set up a rainfly when in a downpour can result in a very wet tent immediately after setting it up. If the inside of your single-wall tent is wet from either condensation or other moisture, it will get the floor of your tent wet once you collapse it down. Double-wall tents tend to be heavier as well. Our four-person tent had a completely mesh upper and had to be set up before we could put the rainfly over it. The result? A small pool of water on the inside of our tent that we had to deal with before we could get out of the rain.

Vestibule. Some tents have a small, covered area attached to the tent that can be a great place to store dirty shoes or wet gear outside of your tent but in a rain-protected area.

Weight and Cost. These two elements tend to share an inverse relationship. As weight increases, price typically decreases. Heavier, more durable fabrics used to mass-produce tents for big-box stores keeps costs down and customer returns to a minimum. Today, there are fabrics available on the market that are significantly lighter than those traditional materials, but they also can be pricier.

Season. Knowing where and when you will be backpacking will help you determine if you need a three- or four-season tent. Three-season tents are generally used in summer and some of the shoulder seasons of spring and fall when temperatures and conditions are milder. Some can handle a few inches of snow. These tents are generally lighter and more breathable than their four-season counterparts. But if you're planning to camp in the snow or in areas with more extreme weather, a four-season (or winter) tent is probably a better fit.

The first tent that we used as a family was a four-person, three-season tent that we purchased at a big-box sale for $20. When we bought it, one of the poles was damaged and there was a tear in the rainfly from the pole breaking through in a large windstorm. We cut off the broken piece of pole and mended the rainfly with some nylon tape.

It definitely wasn't the lightest piece of gear, weighing in at over eight pounds, but with two young children, we weren't hiking very far. What made it great was that it had plenty of headroom, lots of breathability, and was simple to set up. When it was empty, I could unzip the door, pick it up by the frame, lift it over my head, and easily shake out all the dirt, sand, and mess that comes with camping with toddlers and kids.

Kaleo (age 2) poking his head out of our four-person tent on our first backpacking trip. Notice that the tent didn't fit in the tent pad on one corner and other corner is held down by a rock.

Tarp Tents

When our kids got older and our backpacking trips got longer, we looked for ways to lighten our gear. We opted to start using two ultralight tarp tents. These tents are essentially a single wall of silicone-impregnated nylon (sil nylon) separating you from the elements. Ours weighed in at just 34 ounces (or slightly over two pounds) each. By carrying two of these instead of one big four-person tent, we were able to eliminate four pounds from our pack!

A tarp tent is basically the opposite of our four-person tent. It is not roomy, but it is easy to set up in the rain because it consists of a single wall with no mesh to let water in. It is also a bit

Hammocks and Bivys and Tarps, Oh My!

There are options for everyone out there.

HAMMOCKS Hammocks keep you off the hard ground and are also nice because you don't need as flat of an area to set up on. However, they limit you to places with trees.

BIVY SACKS Bivy sacks are like tiny tents, big enough to put your sleeping bag in, and they keep the bug net/tent material off your face, but that's about it. Since this is a family backpacking book and bivy sacks are typically made for one person, I won't go into detail here. But know that they could be an option for your kids once they are teens and want to carry their own sleep system to have some privacy.

TARPS Tarps are an excellent, lightweight, affordable option. They do require some skill in setting up to avoid noisy flapping all night long and proper protection from the elements. For bugs, you can use either a smaller bug net to cover your upper body (since your lower body will probably be in a sleeping bag) or a larger bug net to act similarly to the interior mesh of a double-wall tent.

more delicate. It is not freestanding and needs a trekking pole and guylines to stand. But we find that their smaller footprints make it easier to squeeze them into tight spaces in the back-country as opposed to needing to find a site big enough for a four-person tent.

The kids loved having their own tent where they got to whisper and giggle and shove and argue until we threatened to take away their reward jelly beans the next day. (More on the jelly beans and rewards system in Chapter 11.) One evening, they decided to dress up their water bottles using their spare clothing and gave them personalities and acted out silly plays. Dave and I loved having our own tent because on a long camping trip, we are with our kids 24/7 with zero space, and sometimes just having an illusion of separation really helps with sanity. Also, our kids thrash in their sleep. It's nice not getting kicked throughout the night.

4

Clothing

WHEN GOING FOR A BACKPACKING TRIP, predicting what clothing you'll need based on the expected terrain, weather, and temperature is tricky—but crucial. Research your hike and be aware of the potential weather you could encounter on your journey. In this section, I will make sure you're able to be the smug family that says, "There's no such thing as bad weather, just bad gear." Your family may not be thrilled to be out there in the rain or heat, but they *will* be prepared and more comfortable because of it. Let's start with the basics.

THE BASICS

Having a proper clothing-layering system is essential. It is important to know what materials and layers you think you will need based on the season and climate you will be backpacking in. The good news is that with thoughtful layering, you really won't need to pack a lot to handle the majority of weather conditions you may find yourself in.

The typical three-layer system includes a base layer, a mid-layer, and an outer layer. The base layer is directly against your skin. It should be designed to move moisture off your body (a process known as wicking), thus helping you maintain a comfortable body temperature. The mid-layer offers insulation and provides warmth, protecting you from the cold. Finally, the outer layer should provide protection from wind and rain.

To better understand how these layers should function and what kinds of fabrics work best, let's look at sections of the body and break things down layer by layer.

Layering for the Upper Body

Underwear. If you or your child wear bras or other tight under-clothes on top, it is important to make sure the fabric won't rub and that it breathes well. I recommend bringing two bras in total, one in the pack and one on the body. You can wash the previous day's garment early in the day and hang it on your pack to dry (more on washing in Chapter 13). If you're in a dry climate, you'll be able to put a dry one on every day. In a more humid environment, it may take a few days for the band and thicker areas to dry out from sweat or from being washed.

Base-layer shirt. This layer lies against the skin and should be capable of wicking moisture away from your body. Look for shirts that are made of either synthetic or wool. There's a saying in the hiking world: "cotton kills." If you are wearing cotton and it gets wet, it loses its ability to keep you warm or dry, which can have significant consequences in the backcountry. Remember that wetness can come not just from rain, but also from your own perspiration. Wearing clothing with wicking, quick-drying, or insulative-when-wet abilities, such as synthetic or wool, will help you maintain your body temperature more easily.

Synthetic materials wick away moisture and dry quickly but tend to get smelly fast. Wool maintains its insulative properties when wet, keeping you warm in damp conditions, but feels itchy to some people. Wool tends to deal better with foul body smells as well. Try things on and see what works for you and your children. Some people prefer long-sleeve, loose button-down shirts for sun or bug protection. When we hiked the PCT, we hiked with a man who wore such a shirt, and it had a huge zipper pocket on the front where he carried his maps and compass. We gave him the trail name Pouch!

Also included in the base layer should be a long-underwear top in case of colder weather. This can double as a pajama top or spare clothing if your primary clothes get wet.

Mid-layer. An insulating mid-layer can be fleece or a lightweight jacket or vest, or when summer camping, a thicker thermal shirt. As with the base layer, wool and synthetic fabrics typically work well for this layer. When camping in warmer areas, our kids sometimes bring thicker long-sleeve shirts rather than fleece, which they layer over short-sleeve shirts and under jackets.

Kaleo (5) hiking up to the Continental Divide in his layers: synthetic jacket over his light wind jacket and shirt, beanie, and mittens.

Outer layer. The outer layer should provide protection from cold temperatures, wind, and rain. Thin nylon wind jackets, warm hats, gloves or mittens, and a neck gaiter (a thin circular piece of fabric that can be worn a variety of ways to protect the face and neck) are all critical in protecting from the elements. We don't use waterproof jackets (see p. 71 for details on our rain-gear system), but other hikers like them. A warm thermal jacket completes the setup. We've been in snowstorms and hailstorms where a thick long-sleeve shirt under a wind jacket wasn't enough, so we bring whatever thick jackets we have.

When purchasing a warm jacket, consider a bright color (bonus points for hunter's orange) as it makes it easier to see

Layering Reality Check

I know I just talked about the perils of cotton in the backcountry, but here's the reality: on many of our early family backpacking trips, our kids wore whatever shirts were in their bureaus, even if the shirts were cotton. When they were under the age of 6, we'd pack a spare shirt in case they played a little too intensely in the lake or river and got soaked. As we started going on longer trips and needed to get pack weight down, we eliminated one of the shirts, knowing that other items (such as the long-underwear top) could stand in while waiting for the shirt to dry.

As for base layers, after using smelly synthetic for years, I invested in a merino wool sports bra and wool short-sleeve base-layer shirt and have been impressed with their ability to minimize odor after multiple days on the trail.

When it comes to shopping, you'll find thermal base layers at many stores; however, we have found name-brand tops and bottoms for the kids at thrift stores from time to time. Well worth checking out given the cost-savings!

Jackets? When the kids were little, their jacket was whatever synthetic Colorado winter coat they had. The coats would be bulky, but they did the trick and kept them warm. We constantly keep our eyes open at secondhand stores and online resale sites for quality, warm jackets. If you buy them big, the kids can use them for a few years! When you start going for longer distances, you will want to get decent quality that can compress and is lightweight.

your kid on the hike and easier to quickly find the jacket in the pack. See the sleeping bag section for a discussion of the pros and cons of synthetic versus down fill (p. 45)—the same conversations of weight, bulk, and price point apply to jackets.

If you're camping where you know it'll be warm, use your judgment and potentially eliminate the winter coat from your pack. I find that I almost always use mine, so I rarely won't pack it; however, my husband hardly ever uses his, so it is a space and weight saver to consider in the right conditions.

Layering for the Lower Body

Underwear. If you or your child wears tight underclothes, it is important to make sure the fabric breathes and doesn't rub. Boxer briefs are particularly good for long hiking days, as they can eliminate chafing of the inner thighs. As for how many, bring the amount you'll need in order to have a clean option daily. Some backpackers manage this with two to three pairs, with one on, one ready to go, and a third that they will clean in the next day or so. For kids, three to five pairs are great. You never know what they'll sit in or do, and no one likes hiking in damp underwear. If you're in a dry climate, you'll be able to put a dry pair on every day. If you're in a more humid environment, know that it may take a couple of days for the band and thicker areas to dry out from sweat or washing, so an extra pair can be nice.

Base layer. Hikers can enjoy the outdoors in a wide variety of base layers: long pants, leggings, shorts, kilts, or a personal favorite, skirts. Whichever you choose, look for something abrasion resistant, flexible, and with functional pockets (pockets aren't critical when kids are younger, but quick-drying, light, and comfortable are key at any age).

Even in warmer climates, lightweight pants work well, as they reduce sun exposure, protect against bugs, and keep your legs cleaner. Convertible pants are a nice option when temperatures vary, but make sure they don't chafe. My son wore convertible pants on our Tahoe Rim Trail thru-hike, and the zippers rubbed the back of his knees raw when they were in shorts mode. It was also difficult to get the pant legs zipped back on in a hurry, which was a problem when we were suddenly swarmed by mosquitoes. On the other hand, my daughter's convertible pants rolled up easily, with a button to hold them in the capri setting. It was a piece of cake for her to unroll them when in mosquito territory and roll them back up if she was hot.

Leggings can be comfortable to hike in, but they will not protect against mosquitoes and chafing can sometimes be a

PRO TIP

BE SURE TO TAKE NEW CLOTHING out on day hikes or wear it around the house prior to your backpacking trip to check fit and comfort. Pay particular attention to the waistband to get an idea of how it will interact with a backpack's hip belt to minimize pressure points or sore spots. Quick-drying fabrics are ideal. Chafing can be an uncomfortable problem, so also pay attention to any rubbing.

problem if they are not seamless. Finally, long underwear makes a good base layer (and can be reused as pajama bottoms).

Mid-layer. Track pants or athletic pants with elastic waistbands make excellent lightweight, quick-drying options and can often be found in secondhand or big-box stores for a reasonable price. They should be loose enough to go easily over your shoes and base layer.

Easy on-off is helpful for cool mornings. You can keep them on as you eat breakfast, break camp, and start the day's hike, and then easily slip them off and stuff them into your pack as the day warms. A pair with ankle zippers makes it very easy to pull them on and off over shoes. Soccer and athletic joggers often have this option. A pocket is great to have too, but not necessary. Remember, all these features add weight to your clothing.

Outer layer. Nylon wind pants with zippers at the ankles offer protection from wind, rain, mosquitoes, and poky underbrush you may end up bushwhacking through. This layer can be worn alone or layered over other layers for even more warmth.

GEAR TO SUIT THE WEATHER

Now that you have an understanding of the basic clothing systems, it is time to level up and discuss fine-tuning your selections. Let's take a look at some of the weather you may encounter on your adventure and the gear you'll want to have along.

Sun

A **sunhat with a brim** is very helpful on the trail. Whether it is one with a brim that goes all the way around or one that has a flap down the neck and a strap under the chin, it will offer good overall protection from the sun. If you choose to wear a **baseball-style cap** with a forward-facing brim, consider tucking a **bandanna** under the hat to drape down your neck and over your ears when the sun is particularly strong. This setup can shield you from mosquitoes as well.

Sunglasses are valuable for eye protection. In climates from the desert to the snow, it can literally be painful to hike with all the reflected glare, and sunburned eyes are a real health concern.

Protecting the skin from the sun is crucial, but carrying a bottle of sunscreen is heavy and impractical. Additionally, sunscreen is tricky to wash off bodies daily before climbing into sleeping systems and, unless you're purchasing the "reef safe" stuff, isn't great for nature's water systems either. While we typically carry a **travel-size sunscreen** with us, we rely more on items such as **long sleeves**, **umbrellas**, and even **gloves** to protect our skin.

Rain

First, know that it's basically impossible to stay completely dry when hiking through the rain, no matter what system you have. But some choices will be better than others. What you bring should depend on what sort of storms you expect on your trip. Extended days of rain? **Rain jackets** are worthwhile. The occasional summer thunderstorm? Something less may be appropriate, such as a poncho or lighter-weight wind jacket and umbrella combo. Be aware that in wooded or tight areas, loosely flapping ponchos can get snagged easily and jackets could be a better option. The water that accumulates on the brush on either side of the trail can contribute much more to your wetness than what is falling out of the sky. The main goal is not necessarily to keep you completely dry, but to have a system that keeps you warm if/when it gets wet and will dry quickly once the storm passes.

On many of our hikes, each of us would carry an **umbrella**, as well as lightweight, quick-drying nylon **wind pants and jackets**. The umbrella offers excellent protection from not only sun and rain, but also hail! We've been caught in some nasty summer hailstorms in the Rockies and were thankful for the protection of our umbrellas. The wind pants and jackets provide a layer of protection from the rain, and when we do end up getting wet, they dry quickly. We are usually able to continue hiking through the storm with our umbrella and wind gear, which keeps our body temperatures up.

One alternative to our setup is to bring **waterproof jackets and pants**. The drawback to these items is that they are usually heavier, and they don't breathe. If you continue hiking in a rainstorm in clothing that doesn't breathe, you will begin to sweat and may end up just as wet from the inside (and consequently cold). Some waterproof items lose their waterproofness after a certain amount of wear, so be sure to do your due diligence before you leave home if your waterproof gear has seen some wear.

Dave, Rae, and Kaleo hunkered down in a Colorado summertime hailstorm.

Rain skirts provide a happy middle ground between traditional waterproof pants and wind pants. A rain skirt is a lightweight piece of waterproof fabric that wraps around the front of the body and clasps in the back. It should extend from the waist to just below the knees. The skirts I recently made for our family are fastened with Velcro at the waist and left open down the back of the legs for ventilation and to allow unrestricted movement. There are also companies that sell affordable full-body rain gear options. Be aware that you may end up sweating a lot if the ventilation isn't great in these suits. Rain **ponchos** offer great ventilation and can be used over a pack as well. They are also super lightweight and compact.

Note that if the rainstorm comes with a lot of wind, this may affect your rain gear choices. A blustery rainstorm makes everything more challenging. Hiking in a blowing or driving rain with an umbrella is incredibly frustrating (especially with children who aren't as seasoned at angling the umbrella into the wind), and ponchos can blow and flap like crazy. If a storm does kick up that is that bad, consider heading for cover under some trees, sit or crouch down on some sheltered boulders, and create a fort with your umbrellas and have a snack break until the storm lightens up or passes (see p. 163 for lightning safety). Or set up your tent and hang out inside where it is nice and dry. We've done both (the umbrella fort and setting up a tent), and the kids roll with it as part of the backpacking experience.

Keeping your gear dry in the rain is not easy, but **trash-compactor bags** make fairly durable liners inside your pack to protect your sleeping bag and other gear. These bags, designed for trash-compactor machines, are thicker and more hardy than regular trash bags. You can use one trash-compactor bag for your sleeping bag (if you don't have a waterproof stuff sack for your sleeping bag) and another for everything else in your pack. To keep exterior pack pockets dry, you can use a trash bag (though they can be tricky to keep positioned properly) or pack cover, but it requires stopping to put it on in a storm.

Wind

Lightweight, nylon wind jackets and pants will be one of the most beneficial pieces of gear in your pack when it comes to wind. Because they are not waterproof, they will breathe and thus can be worn in warmer windy temperatures without too much discomfort. In addition to cutting the wind, they are bug proof, are sun proof, and can shield you from wet, scratchy brush along the trail. Once the wind lets up and the sun comes back out, these garments tuck easily back in your pack.

Snow

Gear for snow is not much different from what has already been mentioned in other weather conditions. If hiking in extended lower temperatures, you'll want to make sure you have a warm base and a good mid-layer to wear under your coat. Layers are critical in colder temps as your body temperature will fluctuate drastically when hiking or resting. Umbrellas can be nice to hike with when walking on snow as well, as they keep the snow and glare from getting in your eyes.

Outfitting Growing Kids

Kids are constantly growing, typically until some point in high school. Replacing all the gear that they outgrow gets costly quickly, so it is important to shop smart. We've found thrift stores and military-surplus stores to be treasure troves of trail finds. Look there for basic athletic wear, such as soccer shorts or warm-up pants with zippered ankles, which make great light-weight hiking options.

Online marketplaces offer ways to expand your search if you're seeking a specific piece of gear. Big-box stores usu-ally have "garage sales" a few times a year where you can find amazing deals for pricey gear that has perhaps been returned by a customer or shows slight wear and tear or minor defects. Discount outdoor gear retailers are another place to check for inexpensive gear.

Some outdoor stores rent gear. If you're not sure your family is going to make a habit of outdoor exploration, consider renting some gear to test-drive the idea first. Sometimes this gear will be the sturdier and heavier types, but it's an option for just trying it out before making a commitment.

Finally, if you have the time and inclination, you can make your own gear! There are online resources for buying the latest and greatest outdoor fabrics and sewing your own clothing, tents, quilts, and more. You'll find links in the back of the book to some resources that I've used.

Once your kids stop growing, or for gear that doesn't get outgrown easily, look for quality gear that lasts instead of focusing solely on budget. A quality sleeping bag or tent that will last can be a wise investment and cheaper in the long run than replacing it multiple times. A neck warmer made of quality fabrics will be used for years, as will a good headlamp. Socks are crucial when you're walking for miles, and they are not quickly outgrown, so consider a high-quality pair that will last. The point is, sometimes it is worth it to spend a little extra and not have to replace it due to poor manufacturing, heavy weight, or breakage in a year or so.

5

Footwear

JUST LIKE IN THE OLD SONG, (some) boots *are* made for walking. But you can walk in shoes too! Whether boots or shoes, what's really important is that they fit, are comfortable, and can withstand the miles. Your feet take the brunt of the impact on the trail, so it is important to treat them with the care and gear they deserve. Uncomfortable or poorly fitting shoes can make a hike miserable and potentially cut it short. But what exactly should you look for in a good pair of shoes? This section is aimed at helping you figure out how to find your family's perfect fit.

TRAIL SHOES AND BOOTS

When it comes to covering miles on the trail, there are two main types of footwear: trail running shoes and hiking boots. But which to choose? Both have their advantages.

A massive benefit of having a system of lightweight gear is that you are able to wear lightweight shoes on your trip, which minimizes leg fatigue. Trail runners are breathable sneakers with good tread and a somewhat stiffer interior than road-running shoes. They can be more affordable than boots, take less time to break in, and usually result in fewer blisters. A decent pair of trail runners can last 500 miles or more before needing to be replaced.

Boots are appropriate for really difficult, rocky trails. They also work particularly well on consistently wet and muddy trails. The downside is that heavy-duty hiking boots can weigh a pound or more each! That's quite a workout for your legs considering the number of steps you'll take in a day. They can also be quite hot and take a while to dry if you cross a stream in them.

The same applies to shoes and boots for kids. Kids' footwear, just like adult footwear, can get really pricey, really fast. We try to keep things affordable but comfortable. When our kids were young (ages 2 to 5), we'd have them hike in whatever sneakers or shoes they wore for daily use. This included a mix of hand-me-downs, decent brand-name shoes from secondhand stores, or affordable new shoes from big-box stores.

When our daily mileage got longer (consistently more than 5 miles per day for multiple days in a row), we looked for their first pair of "real" hiking shoes. That's where things got a little trickier.

Let's take a closer look at the four things we always look for in hiking shoes—whether boots or trail runners—for the kids.

IF YOU GET ONTO A LONG TRAIL and your kid starts complaining about something rubbing funny somewhere, consider cutting out padding from the insole to eliminate hotspots. You can do it to your shoe too. Our feet are all unique, and sometimes a bit of adjusting can help the shoe fit.

Good fit/comfort. Have your kids with you to try shoes on and make sure they are comfortable. It can be tricky to get kids to turn their attention away from things like colors and style and focus on comfort. Trying to get a straight answer out of a 5- or 6-year-old about how a shoe feels can be an arduous process. We have tried on every shoe in stores with no luck because the tongue felt funny or there was something poking somewhere. Just keep trying, or maybe try on another day when the kids are in better moods.

Too much choice can be overwhelming. You can simplify the process by buying them a pair of shoes that meet your criteria and bringing them home for the kids to try on. It is wise to find out a store's return policy. Some places let you return them only if you test them indoors, and other places will let you return them even if you go for a hike outdoors as long as they aren't damaged or dirty.

No waterproofing. Kids love nothing more than tromping through water. Hikes can also involve stream crossings, where the water is high enough to go over the top of the shoe and

Rae and Kaleo hiking up some snow on the Tahoe Rim Trail, Nevada, in trail runners. Rae has low gaiters on, and her camp shoes are hanging on the side of her pack.

above the ankle. When water gets that high, it goes into the shoe, soaking the foot, sock, and shoe interior. Shoes that aren't waterproof are more breathable and dry much more quickly than waterproof shoes, as waterproofing tends to hold moisture in. That same breathability prevents feet from sweating as much as they would in a waterproof shoe. Yet it is surprisingly difficult to find kid's hiking shoes that are not waterproof.

All that said, waterproof boots come in handy when trekking through damp areas with lots of mud. If that describes trails on your trip, trust your gut and go with a waterproof boot rather than a trail runner for your kids. But consider taking off their boots and putting on their camp shoes for stream crossings. (See the weight categories chart in the appendix on p. 190 to see how shoe weight factors in to gear weight.)

Tread. Decent tread is essential for gripping rocks and getting through mud, snow, and ice. For us, this requirement eliminated all the flat-bottomed sneakers that our kids use daily at school and that we use for gym workouts. We've found that trail runners have excellent tread, which narrowed the buying field significantly.

Laces (not Velcro). Velcro is commonly used in smaller-size shoes. Sometimes it is a single strap near the top of the shoe; sometimes it is multiple straps. After hiking through mud, water,

Footwear Takeaways

▸ Have your kids with you to try shoes on and make sure they are comfortable! (My kids say this is priority number one.)

▸ Will you be in water that is likely to go over the top of the shoe? If so, avoid waterproofing to help expedite drying.

▸ Look for tread that offers good grip when walking on snow, granite, and smooth rocks.

▸ Make sure the laces aren't so thick that they won't stay tied but aren't so thin that they hurt little fingers trying to tighten them.

dirt, and sand, Velcro loses its ability to fasten and creates a tripping hazard because the shoe will no longer properly stay on. Avoid Velcro once you start going on more serious hikes. Also, beware of shoes that have quick-lacing systems involving skinny, wirelike laces and a pull tab. My kids loved these shoes, but after five or more days of hiking, cinching up the laces started hurting their fingers. We've stuck with regular-thickness laces ever since.

CAMP SHOES

While camp shoes are technically a "nice to have," I tend to put them in the "must have" column of our packing lists. When backpacking, sometimes feet get wet. Maybe it is from a stream crossing or maybe it is just from sweat, but however it happens, there is a good chance that you'll want to air out your feet throughout the day to avoid any maladies associated with damp feet. In our family, every two hours or so, we take a "shoes-off" break to allow our feet to breathe and air out.

Once we reach our campsite for the night, we do the same. During this time, the kids love playing and exploring as soon as they're not encumbered by their packs and are allowed to roam off the trail a bit. Camp shoes, which are super easy to slip on while socks and hiking shoes are drying, are perfect for these times! They offer just enough protection that the kids can play without getting something stuck in their foot but are open enough that their feet have a chance to dry out. We have found over years of hiking that this has really helped us to maintain good foot health. We also use this shoes-off time to check out any hot spots (areas of irritation on the foot that are getting rubbed the wrong way) and make sure to treat them to prevent blisters (by adding duct tape or moleskin to the spot, or cutting out the piece of shoe that is rubbing the foot incorrectly).

Since you will be carrying your camp shoes on your back while hiking, it's important to make sure they are lightweight. For us, slip-on, foam clogs fit the bill. They are fine to use in water, the heel strap makes it easy to attach them to our packs, we can wear them with socks if it is cold out, and they are featherlight. Others prefer strappy water sandals as their camp shoes. They are heavier to carry, and toe straps prevent sock wearing, but if you already have these shoes and like them, great. Just be cognizant of weight on the pack.

Gaiters

Hiking gaiters keep rocks, sand, and debris out of shoes and socks, which means cleaner, happier feet. Traditional gaiters can be heavy and hot so are not ideal for lightweight backpacking. Some companies offer modern gaiters made of lightweight material, such as Lycra. Designed mainly for trail runners, these usually hook to your shoelaces and Velcro to the back of your shoes. They come up to the lower calf, just high enough to protect the opening of your shoes from pebbles and dirt.

6

Other Gear

WITH CLOTHING, SHOES, and the Big Three out of the way, let's focus on other key equipment to consider. Every piece of gear in your pack will serve a need on the trail. There are lots of blogs, videos, and websites with lists ranging from general backpacking gear to trail-specific gear (search "PCT gear list" as an example). There are also many sources to research every item and yet more websites to find the best prices for gear. I personally enjoy going into a store to check out the pieces in person (online pictures can be deceiving, and it's tough to gauge size), but sometimes for more niche items, buying online makes the most sense. In this section, I will go over what works for us. Feel free to improvise and modify these lists as needed for your family.

COOKING SYSTEMS

Mealtimes bring families together. Literally. Huddled around one pot, shoulder to shoulder, taking turns (or squabbling) over who gets the next bite. The lightest option we have found is cooking our meal in one large titanium pot, and everyone taking turns digging their spoon in. For the purpose of this section, a cooking system is generally made up of a stove and fuel, cook pot, cups/bowls (if you use them), and eating utensils. Depending on the size of your family and how much each member eats, you may find yourselves needing to alter your cooking system.

With the increase in forest fires across the Western US, cooking over an open campfire is no longer the option it once was, so let's look at more contained solutions. Stoves are usually categorized by fuel type: white gas, propane, solid-fuel tablet, and alcohol. The biggest difference between white gas and propane is the container it comes in. Propane requires a stronger, heavier container for the pressurized fluid. These containers make it tricky to gauge how much fuel is left. White gas containers are usually refillable; propane containers aren't. The downside to white gas is that it is more finicky and requires priming. Propane is simpler—just turn it on and light it. It is important to check on fuel availability at resupply stops. Propane is typically the most accessible, with white gas the second most common. The downside of propane is the waste created by the spent canisters.

Alcohol stoves are incredibly light (some are even made from only an old soda can). The fuel is denatured alcohol, often found in hardware stores. The downside to this type of stove is that

Our one-pot meal on Isle Royale, Michigan.

more and more places are banning them because of spill and fire dangers. They are also increasingly prohibited during times of open-flame bans as well, due to high fire danger. There is no way to simmer; they are either on or off. Once you light it, it burns until it runs out of fuel. Finally, the fuel itself is not very powerful, which means energy per ounce is really low, so it doesn't burn very hot. This means cook times are longer.

Whichever type of stove you use, windscreens are usually included and are a key component to keeping heat focused under the pot and protected.

Pots and Utensils

As for what to cook your delicious food in, titanium pots are the lightest (but most expensive) cook pots. They are stronger than aluminum, much lighter than steel, and transfer heat quickly.

Stainless steel pots are a heavier but more affordable option. They are sturdy and more scratch-resistant than titanium, but they don't conduct heat evenly, which can lead to hot spots. Aluminum is a great midpoint option, conducting heat evenly and quickly. They are lighter than steel but heavier than titanium.

Finding a pot with a lid will speed up boil times and reduce fuel use. As for size, when just my husband and I backpacked, we used a 0.9-liter pot. Now we use a 1.9-liter pot with our two kids. For larger families, multiple cookpots may be necessary.

When it comes to utensils, spoons are all you really need. Sporks can work too. Make sure you have one sturdy, larger spoon to do the cooking and stirring. For the rest of the family, thick plastic spoons work well. We found the perfect utensils at a local frozen yogurt shop, with the bonus of them all being different colors, so it is easy to tell whose is whose.

PRO TIP

IF YOU WANT TO GO AS LIGHTWEIGHT on equipment as possible, consider going stoveless (cookless) entirely. It cuts down on weight and hassle, eliminating the need for not only a stove, but also for fuel and a pot. This option works best for shorter trips as cold, uncooked meals for days on end can end up being unsatisfying for some. Note that any dehydrated food can be rehydrated using a cold-soak method. For example, ramen noodles take three minutes to soften when cooked, but can soften when soaked for fifteen minutes as well!

WATER PURIFICATION

Filters and chemicals are the most common options for water purification when filling up in the backcountry; some people use ultraviolet light filters too. **Hand-pump filters** will leave your water tasting fresh, but can clog and involve more time and energy. While there are some lighter-weight filters these days, many are still fairly heavy. There are small, light **squeeze-bag** options that have you physically rolling up a bag filled with water to push it through a filter. If you're filling four or more water bottles at a time, however, this option is time-consuming and can be cold depending on where you're pulling water from and how often you need to refill the bag.

Larger **gravity bags** allow you to fill up a bag with several liters at a time, hang it in a tree, and let gravity do the work of pulling the water through the filter. The larger gravity bag systems are heavier than the smaller squeeze bags, but only require one fill-up from the river and you can head back to camp. With the smaller bags, you need to stay by the water as it will take many refills to take care of the whole family's supply.

Chemical treatments, like iodine drops or small amounts of bleach, are lighter than filtration systems, but can change the taste of the water, which some kids may struggle with. Another downside is that if you're pulling water from a source with lots of particulate matter, you're going to have all that bonus content in your bottles, which can make even adults question their life choices. I have definitely gazed longingly at folks with filters while scooping water directly from some such floatie-filled

Treating water from a lake on Isle Royale, Michigan.

ponds. Telling myself that their filters get clogged and need replacing helped only moderately.

While I don't have a solution for getting all the floaties out of water bottles (other than perhaps filtering it with a clean bandanna), we can do something about the chemical taste: add a sport-hydration tablet to the water after it is treated. Our kids love the treat of having fizzy water in the backcountry, and we like that it encourages them to stay hydrated.

NAVIGATION

Be sure to bring tools for navigation as well as back-up plans. There are many **trail apps** that will show where you are on a trail along with all the pertinent info of how much farther you have before water or other milestones and what your elevation is. Cal-Topo, Gaia GPS, and Topo Maps US are examples of such apps. **Physical maps** have been go-to resources for hundreds of years and still have their place in the backpacks of hikers around the world today. It's a good idea to carry a paper map in case your electronic navigation device loses battery power or gets dropped into water. Another important tool for navigation is the **compass**. Be sure to bring one on every trip and know how to use it.

We use a combination of navigational tools. Our primary tool is a physical topographic map with trails and physical features of the area clearly displayed. If we are wondering if we're on the wrong trail or trying to get an idea of where we are on the map, we can access our backup tool—our **phone**. The US Topo Maps app shows our elevation, which can help us place ourselves on the physical map. We always bring a compass to confirm directions when we are hiking, which is especially helpful in new areas. To conserve battery life, we keep the phone on airplane and bat-tery-saver mode the whole hike and turn it off at night. The app will give us GPS coordinates and elevation in airplane mode. If we are out for longer than four days, we will bring a portable charger to keep the phone alive. Some people use solar chargers.

Out on a hike, be sure to involve the kids with routefind-ing and navigation by having them look for landmarks that are represented on the page. Remember that technology can fail (dead batteries, water damage, etc.), so having a physical map is an excellent way to stay oriented in the backcountry.

Satellite Messengers and Personal Locator Beacons

As you head deeper into the backcountry on longer trips, you could research getting a satellite messenger or personal locator beacon. Satellite messengers can allow for one- and two-way messaging (perfect for letting folks know you're okay if you haven't hit your destination yet). Some offer tracking and SOS messaging if you're in need of a rescue. The service is not inexpensive, but if you're going into the great outdoors more regularly, it can bring everyone peace of mind to know that you can reach help (and have two-way communication) if things go awry and you're away from cell service. Personal locator beacons are much more specific: they have just one button, and when activated during an emergency, send your location information to search and rescue.

Resources and Training

Finally, as mentioned in the Introduction, I highly recommend if you're heading into the backcountry, especially with children, that you take a Wilderness First Aid course. They are offered in most areas by organizations such as Colorado Mountain Club, National Outdoor Leadership School (NOLS), Wilderness Medicine, Stonehearth Open Learning Opportunities (SOLO), and many others. The time commitment is usually brief—often only a weekend of your time—and will provide lots of hands-on training from experienced instructors, including CPR and epinephrine (EpiPen) certifications. NOLS and the Red Cross offer first aid classes to give you an in-depth understanding and training for a variety of issues that could arise on a backpacking trip.

NOLS also offers a *Wilderness Medicine Pocket Guide* that you can carry in your first aid kit, the more thorough classic *Wilderness Medicine Field Guide*, and the bestselling *NOLS Wilderness Medicine* book. Those are just a few of the many great books on the subject.

I cannot stress enough the importance of getting trained so you're able to keep your head about you if there is an injury in the field. Even though the majority of the treatment procedures for larger injuries are basically "stabilize and get help," it is beneficial to know the various stabilization methods and how to transport a person out of a trail.

For more information about courses on wilderness training and other safety courses, please see the "Helpful Resources" in the back of the book.

Kits and Checklists

It is a good idea to carry a utilities kit, fire-starter kit, first aid kit, toiletries kit, bathroom kit, and menstruation kit in your pack. We keep ours in quart-size zipper freezer bags that are a little sturdier than the regular zipper bags. Be sure to check these kits before every big trip to ensure you have everything on your list and that nothing has expired or run out. Another helpful item is a fifty-foot length of rope or paracord. It can be used to hang food or as a laundry line if your things get wet. Here is what we have in our kits.

FIRE STARTER KIT

- ☐ Dryer lint or cotton balls
- ☐ Waterproof matches
- ☐ Birthday candles (stay lit and are easy to hold longer than a match)
- ☐ Lighter
- ☐ Waterproof container
- ☐ Q-tips dipped in Vaseline

UTILITIES KIT

- ☐ Multitool knife
- ☐ Sewing needle and thread, safety pins
- ☐ Patch kit for inflatable sleeping pads, tents, clothing, and gear
- ☐ Duct tape (wrapped around a piece of cardboard or old credit card)

- ☐ Zip ties
- ☐ Safety pins
- ☐ Compass (and know how to use it)

TOILETRIES KIT

- ☐ Lip balm (with SPF rating)
- ☐ Small bottle bug spray
- ☐ Small bottle sunscreen
- ☐ Toothbrushes
- ☐ Toothpaste (travel size)
- ☐ Floss
- ☐ Nail clippers
- ☐ Vaseline
- ☐ Prescription medications
- ☐ Collapsible wash bowl

BATHROOM KIT

- ☐ Toilet paper
- ☐ Empty bag for used toilet paper
- ☐ Hand sanitizer
- ☐ Hand wipes
- ☐ Trowel

MENSTRUATION KIT (see p. 180)

- ☐ Applicator-less tampons
- ☐ Menstrual cup
- ☐ Period panties
- ☐ Hand sanitizer (shared with bathroom kit)

FIRST AID KIT

Carry a first aid kit on every trip. Build the kit around the number of people in your group, where you are going, and what you might encounter. Don't put anything in there that you don't know how to use. NOLS suggests the following items in a first aid kit:

Basic Must-have:

- ☐ 1-inch cloth tape
- ☐ 3-inch conforming roll gauze
- ☐ 3"×4" nonstick gauze pads
- ☐ 4"×4" sterile gauze pads
- ☐ 4"×6" elastic wrap
- ☐ Antibiotic ointment packets
- ☐ Antiseptic towelettes
- ☐ Fabric bandages (1"×3" bandages, plus knuckle/fingertip bandages)
- ☐ Moleskin dressings
- ☐ Nitrile gloves
- ☐ NOLS Wilderness Medicine Pocket Guide
- ☐ Safety pins
- ☐ Sharpie
- ☐ Triangular bandages (large triangle of cloth fabric to create a sling, splint, and more)
- ☐ Tweezers

Additional Items for Those Familiar with its Use:

- ☐ 12cc irrigation syringe
- ☐ 2nd Skin dressings (New-Skin)
- ☐ Coban wrap
- ☐ Oral thermometer
- ☐ Povidone-iodine solution
- ☐ Rescue mask (a plastic barrier with a one-way valve in the middle for CPR use. Protects both parties from transmitting fluids.)
- ☐ SAM splint
- ☐ Sterile scrub brush
- ☐ Tincture of benzoin swabs
- ☐ Transparent film dressings
- ☐ Trauma shears
- ☐ Wound closure strips

PART 3

MOVE

7

Considering Distances

HERE WE ARE, FINALLY READY to put our feet on the trail and *move*! This is the moment you've been visualizing for so long, and you're ready to get some of those glossy photos of your own. One way to make sure the whole family is smiling and enjoying the adventure is to take an honest look at your current lifestyle pretrip. Are you and your kids active and generally healthy? Are you able to carry some weight on your back and walk? Awesome! Backpacking as a family is great because you can tailor it to meet everyone's ability levels. Let's talk distance.

HOW FAR IS FAR ENOUGH?

Every family is different. Some families have backpacked a longer trail, such as the Colorado Trail or the Pacific Crest Trail, with their children. For others, a simple trip of a few miles is enough. For a general frame of reference, some experts have suggested that kids 3 and under can go 0.25 to 2 miles, ages 4 to 7 can go 2 to 4 miles, and ages 8 and up can go 6 to 10 miles a day. Our own family experience generally fell within these guidelines as well.

That said, the reality is that getting toddlers to make continual forward progress in a specific direction can be challenging. Two miles can seem like a hundred. Fits and spurts is the theme for this group. For us, the "hiking" part of the day would last just a few hours and would be filled with stops to smell flowers, look at bugs, and play in the dirt. It definitely is more about enjoying the journey than it is about the destination at this age.

If your child is 4 to 7 years old and you've never been on a backpacking trip, now is the perfect time to start. With kids this age, you're able to tackle slightly longer distances physically. The biggest challenge will be keeping them mentally engaged and ensuring a positive experience. In terms of pace, a good rule of thumb for this age group is averaging about 0.5 to 1 mile per hour, depending on how many breaks you take and what the terrain is like. Slow and steady was always the theme for us when our kids were this age.

For the 8 and older crew, it is easy to get carried away by grandiose dreams of tackling peaks and divides, especially if you've been backpacking for a few years, but remember the kids are still young. You can definitely make it up to those goalposts with training, but make sure they have enough energy to get back down to safety before calling it a night.

By the time your kids become teens, they may start leaving you behind as they head up the trail with a friend, backpacks bobbing along as you catch drifts of giggles on the wind and realize all your efforts have paid off. It is truly magical.

A good way to strengthen your kids' hiking abilities is to go on day hikes. Have them carry a small daypack with their own water or toys, and just see how far they can go. If your kids are whiney or grouchy, don't worry—that's totally normal! Sometimes the transition between whatever they were doing at home and the trail can make for cranky kids. Just realize that if they are able to muddle through 2 to 4 miles on a day hike (understanding that it could take two to four hours to cover those distances), there is a good chance they can get through that and likely more in a day of backpacking.

WALK, BREAK, REPEAT

One reason you can cover more ground when backpacking rather than on a day hike is that you can have seven to eight hours of walking time a day. When you wake up on the trail with everything you need, you have the opportunity to go farther in a day than if you pack from home and drive to the trailhead. You can literally hike until either you are too tired to walk anymore or until the sun sets. Your first and last days will likely be shorter mileages as you need to account for travel time to or from the destination.

We have found that it is pretty hard to hike a kid until they are too tired to walk anymore. They will usually proclaim loudly that they are exhausted and their feet are going to fall off and

After a full day of hiking on the Tahoe Rim Trail in California, the kids practiced skiing in their sneakers while Dave made dinner.

they're about to die, but as soon as you take a rest break to eat, they scamper off to play on the rocks or with water in the stream.

Rarely do they just sit still, eat, and rest for the entire break. This may be more about boredom than fatigue, and I have some suggestions later in the book for how to alleviate some of the complaining (see Chapter 11, "Games and Rewards").

After a brief break, you put your packs back on and continue walking. You do this repeatedly for hours on end, until you reach your predetermined stopping point. Make note, it does take longer to walk through gorgeous areas than it does through less-scenic sections of trail.

Our daily schedule that started when our youngest was around age 5 and could hike for an hour (note that I say he "could" hike for an hour, not that he "wanted" to) looked something like this:

8:00 a.m.	Wake up, eat breakfast, pack up.
9:30 a.m.	Start hiking.
10:30–10:45 a.m.	Short break and snack.
11:45 a.m.–12:45 p.m.	Longer (shoes-off) break and bigger snack.
1:45–2:00 p.m.	Short break and snack.
3:00–3:15 p.m.	Short break and snack.
4:30–6:00 p.m.	Longer break, cook dinner.
7:00 p.m.	Stop for the day, set up camp.

Our youngest is now a teen, and we still follow this schedule for the most part. Sometimes we're able to start walking earlier or walk till later in the day, but this remains our general guide. A "short break" is about 15 minutes or so and is a chance to sit, take off the pack, have some snacks and water, and chat. A longer, "shoes-off break" is 30 minutes to an hour, offering the

PRO TIP

DO "DINNER" FOR LUNCH. If you know you are coming up on a long, waterless stretch, and you hit the last water source earlier in the day the day, consider cooking your dinner meal then and having dry snacks at traditional dinnertime. Flexibility is key when backpacking.

Setting Distances and Expectations

▸ **Distance and pace largely depend on the age of your kids.**
We've gone anywhere from 1.5 miles (when our youngest
was 2.5) to 17 miles (when our youngest was 6) in a day
with our kids. The big day was during our Tahoe Rim Trail
hike, and we built up to it. Kids got into a rhythm after that
many consecutive days on the trail, and they were really
motivated to get to town the next day for ice cream.

▸ **Set expectations early on with your kids.** Make it sound
like there isn't an option to quit. Make it a matter of fact that
you are doing this trip.

▸ **Don't be discouraged by crankiness.** Just because kids
are cranky on a day hike or on the first day of a longer
backpacking trip doesn't mean they'll be cranky for the
entire trip. Sometimes it just takes some time to transition.

▸ **Embrace the journey, not just the destination.** When
kids are young, go at a slow pace that allows for frequent
breaks and stopping to smell the flowers.

▸ **Kids don't usually rest at breaks.** They take breaks from
walking to play and explore. As long as they consume
calories while doing whatever they're doing, we usually
are okay with it. Of course, we remind them that "this is a
break for resting!" which we then bring up again when they
complain of being tired when we start hiking. Reliable routines and rewards for milestones (see p. 144) are motivators
you'll need to keep them going at the end of the day.

> ▸ **Consider bail-out options.** For longer trips, it can be good to know in advance what possible bail-out points you have if things go wrong. For example, on a loop trip, are there other trails that cut back to where you started your trip? What about a nearby roadway that allows hitchhiking back to your starting point?

chance to air out the toes. The kids might sit with us, but more often than not, they use this time to play, swim, or explore. We typically try to take these breaks at fun locations, such as a creek crossing, a lake, a big rock outcropping, or a place with a view. We've also taken plenty of breaks just on the side of the trail.

Be flexible and don't be afraid of extending the length of these breaks (within reason, still allowing you to get where you need to go that night). Longer breaks are really where kids just get to be curious kids. This time usually involves a bigger snack as well. After everyone is good and rested, we get our packs back on and continue down the trail.

We gave our kids waterproof digital watches as a gift one year, and my son loved to keep time and let us know when we were coming up on a break. It also helped cut back on his constant "Can we take a break?" lament because he could see the passage of time more clearly. It's easy to lose track of time when you're just walking!

8

Selecting a Campsite

YOU MADE YOUR MILES FOR THE DAY! Your family is happily tired and looking forward to climbing into your comfy sleep systems and relaxing. First things first: finding a spot to rest your heads. This brings us to the adventure of selecting a campsite.

Earlier in the book, we discussed permits and reservations (see p. 15). Depending on the type of trip you are on, your campsite may be designated and specify a tent pad that you must pitch your tent on. Or it may be more flexible, and your campsite's location could be up to you.

EVALUATING YOUR SITE

If you do have flexibility in deciding where to set up your tent for the night, try to get to your stopping point early enough so it is light out when you are evaluating your site. Here are some questions to consider:

Malia and Rae going over the map at our site in the Maroon Bells-Snowmass Wilderness, Colorado. Photo by David Heinrich

- ▸ Can your tent(s) fit in the space?
- ▸ Are you at least 200 feet or more from both the trail and any water source, including creeks, streams, rivers, and lakes?
- ▸ Is there an already-existing campsite that meets the above criteria? Preference should be given to using an existing site over creating a new campsite to help minimize disturbance of pristine areas.
- ▸ Is the ground sloping? A little slope is OK, especially in wet weather. Plan out if you want your head or your feet to be uphill.
- ▸ Does the site have low spots or drainage gullies? These can become pools if it rains. Consider how water will run

through your campsite if it starts to rain while you are inside your tent.

▸ What is surrounding the campsite? Are there dead trees that could fall on your tent if it is windy? Is there a huge rock outcropping to the east that will shade your tent till later in the morning?

▸ What's below your tent? Check for rocks, cactus, or other obstructions.

▸ Where's the wind coming from? If your tent has a lower "foot" portion, have that side facing toward the prevailing wind direction.

▸ What's nearby? Campsites that have something fun for your kids to explore is a bonus. Rock outcroppings, lakes, creeks, and snowbanks are always hits.

▸ What are the current fire regulations for where you are staying? There could be seasonal fire bans in place for a specific region, or oftentimes, popular or sensitive areas may not allow campfires. Check for the latter on your map of the area.

Practice makes perfect, and you'll continue to learn new tips and strategies over time. We've learned that camping on a valley floor is chilly because cold air settles as the night cools. Camping in a meadow can sometimes led to major condensation issues on the inside of a single wall tent. Camping next to lakes and creeks can often be the coldest at night as the cool air settles into the low parts of the area. Sometimes finding a low ridge

PRO TIP

IF YOUR TENT ZIPPER FAILS, skipping teeth and leaving gaps, it is helpful to have a few safety pins in your repair kit to hold it together. When you get home, use needle-nose pliers to pinch the pull back together. For really stubborn zipper fails, a gear repair shop can usually clean and repair, or replace a broken tent zipper.

near a creek or lake can increase the nighttime temperature by a few degrees. Light breezes can help reduce the impact of biting bugs. Duffy beds of pine needles in a forest can make for a warm and cozy night of sleep. Compacted dirt can bend tent stakes as you try to drive them in, so improvise by wrapping your guylines around rocks or filled water bottles and hope for no major wind. Always be aware of cactus, which can poke multiple holes in your sleeping pads.

9

Leave No Trace

SINCE WE ARE DISCUSSING CAMPSITES and moving through these natural areas, it's a good time to examine the seven basic principles of Leave No Trace. These principles vary slightly in name from source to source, but the intent is the same: leave no trace of your presence behind when you move through the wild.

THE SEVEN PRINCIPLES

The Leave No Trace nonprofit organization was formed in 1994 with the goal of educating people on how to help protect the environment. According to their website, an alarming nine out of ten people in the outdoors are uninformed about their impacts, so I am going to discuss the basics here, but be sure to check out lnt.org to learn more.

1. **Plan ahead and prepare.** Planning ahead means checking your route and making sure you know what to do in case of flash floods or inclement weather. Know what fire restrictions are in place. Bring enough water and food and the right gear. Let people know where you're going. Know your pace and give yourselves enough time to get to a safe place to camp for the night.

2. **Travel and camp on durable surfaces.** When you're traveling and camping in high-use areas, stick to designated trails and set up your tent on established tent sites. Practically speaking, this means looking for areas where the vegetative cover has already been lost so you cause no further impact. Stay 200 feet or more away from water sources to preserve wildlife pathways. When going off-trail in pristine areas, try to minimize damage to fragile ecosystems. This means if you're in a meadow, have your family spread out to minimize repeated footsteps in one place. If you're in the desert where there are cryptobiotic (living) soils, walk on rock or in each other's footsteps to minimize harm. Walk on durable surfaces, like sand or rocks, where possible. Leave the area as you found it by fluffing up any vegetation flattened by your tent. Don't tie hammocks to trees with ropes that will damage the trunk or dig trenches around tent sites. Try to have as little impact on an area as possible. Don't break branches from trees, build camp furniture, or let kids carve their names into a tree's bark.

Rae and Malia at our established campsite in the Tetons. Massive muffins make excellent high-calorie meals for the first breakfast on the trail (they tend to get horribly smashed if you try make them last longer than that).

3. **Dispose of waste properly.** I like to think this one is a no-brainer. Whatever you pack in, you pack out. Make sure to pack out even food-scrap waste (including orange peels!). Pack out other trash you find in the wilderness too. And if you're going to the bathroom, make sure you're at least 200 feet from a water source and follow the guidelines outlined in the "Hygiene" section of this book (see Chapter 13).

4. **Leave what you find.** Simply put, don't pack out what you don't bring in. I know, this one is a heartbreaker for kids who love to gather sticks and rocks and other cool things. Our kids are allowed to play with them when we are at a

campsite, but we make sure to leave it there for the next kid (or bird, or animal) to use. If you are consistent with the rules and explain that it is for the animals, your kids will learn how to be great environmental stewards. Take pictures of them holding their favorite stick or rock to let them know you see how special it is.

5. **Minimize campfire impacts.** Campfires can be quite detrimental to the backcountry. They sterilize the ground below them and can be extremely dangerous if the wind picks up or they are left still burning (or warm). For the increasingly arid Western US, think twice about having a campfire. If you're going to be in a designated campsite with an established fire ring, be familiar with any fire bans that are in place. If there is no ban, keep the fire small, using only dead and already-down wood when you are there. Make sure it is dead out before you leave. "Dead out" means that you should feel be able to put your bare hand into the ashes of your campfire before you leave the site. I have come across smoldering, smoking campfires with no humans in sight. In the high country where firewood is scarce, consider not having a fire. We don't usually build campfires in dispersed campsites in the backcountry. We use our stove to cook dinners and save campfires for when we are in an area with an established fire ring. By packing special treats for backpacking that are different from the s'mores the kids get when we go car camping (where there are fire rings and wood avail-

able for purchase), we keep them interested in both types of camping for different reasons.

6. **Respect wildlife.** Keep your distance. Move quietly past ungulates (moose and deer) so you don't startle them. Never approach or try to feed or touch animals. Make some noise so you don't startle a bear. Be smart about your food smells and always store food properly in bear country. See Chapter 10 for more on food storage and other crucial information about dealing with animals.

7. **Be considerate of other visitors.** Help everyone enjoy their outdoor experience. Keep your group as unobtrusive as possible. We're definitely not silent when we walk—we tell stories and sing songs!—but we are close enough to each other that we aren't yelling back and forth up the trail. Show the same respect at your campsite. Be sure you know about any dog regulations during the planning process. If you do

PRO
TIP

PLAY A GAME WITH YOUR KIDS when you are out on the trail using these seven principles. Have them identify examples of people either following the principles or not following them. Or ask them in your own camp and on your hike if you're following them or not following them using examples.

hike with a dog, keep them with you (and obey leash laws). Pay attention to people needing to pass. If you're on a narrow trail heading downhill, move over to let the folks going uphill by. Mountain bikes should yield to both pedestrians and equestrians. Pedestrians yield to equestrians.

PART 4

EAT, DRINK, PLAY

10

Food and Drink on the Trail

HIKING A TRAIL WITH HAPPY KIDS skipping along for hours on end sounds amazing, right? I think so too. I can't guarantee that this book will make it happen, but I can guarantee if you ignore this section that it definitely won't come to fruition. Proper nutrition and hydration are probably the most critical pieces of the happiness puzzle out on the trail, along with appropriate clothing (I got you "covered" on that topic in Chapter 4).

There's a lot to discuss, so let's dive in, with a closer look at hydration on the go.

HYDRATION

As an adult, you have (hopefully) developed a working understanding of the benefits of staying hydrated. It makes us feel better, minimizes headaches, and generally helps us operate more optimally. Kids haven't had that life experience yet and tend to

PRO TIP

IF YOU'RE NOT FAMILIAR with your kids' signs of dehydration yet, track their bathroom breaks on the trail. You can even watch to see how yellow their urine is. The clearer it is, the more hydrated they are.

be reluctant or forgetful when it comes to staying on top of their drinking. This is especially the case when the water is funky tasting or not as clear as they're used to. Compound that with them exerting energy during a hike, and it can lead to dehydration pretty easily.

Maybe your kids won't have this issue, but ours enjoy fighting us on drinking. They neglect to drink, or they don't drink enough, or they insist that they're "*Not thirsty!*" Our daughter's tell is a sigh, a long, deep, mournful one that instantly prompts Dave and I to command, "Drink! Five sips!" When our son starts complaining for a break (before our regularly scheduled hourly breaks), we have him drink more water. There are a surprising number of times that getting them to rehydrate is all it takes to perk up their spirits and get them chattering and walking with vigor again.

A Matter of Taste

As for funky-tasting water, hydration flavor tablets can be a game changer (see p. 90). We let the kids pick a flavor, and we are each allowed one tablet a day (or every other day). This means that one of our waters each day (usually in the afternoon when spirits are beginning to flag) will taste like lightly flavored fizzy water. Oh, the joy and excitement! It is the little things in life when you're backpacking. They definitely help get the kids excited about hydrating.

Water Bottles

For water bottles, we use disposable (recyclable) sports-drink bottles that you can buy for about a dollar at any convenience store. Our main criterion is that the bottle has a wide mouth, making it easy to refill from a variety of water sources. Bottles with smaller openings also tend to freeze more easily on cold nights.

Each person typically carries two bottles. We remove the label on one of the bottles, and it becomes our breakfast shake bottle as well. From about age 5, the kids would carry their own bottles, though we typically wouldn't fill the bottles all the way in order to keep the weight manageable on their shoulders). You'll want to determine the water availability on your route in advance, as additional water storage may be necessary. What is the longest stretch you'll need to go between water refills?

When we get to town, it is easy to replace the water bottles for fresh ones. They end up getting dirty over time, so it is nice to recycle them, and you can get clean ones at almost any store. They are lightweight, inexpensive, and fairly durable. And as a bonus, when you buy a fresh water bottle, you get your choice of beverage included! It always makes heading back out of town more exciting with an icy cold beverage to enjoy on the trail.

Water Sources

On the trail you will probably come across a variety of water sources. Depending on where you are hiking, you may have the luxury of crystal-clear spring water gurgling straight out of a mountainside, or you might be stuck filling up at a stagnant, murky pond. It is always best practice to look for flowing water to fill from, when possible. The smaller the volume of flowing water, the better. Small side trickles and streams can be cleaner than a river or larger creek.

When filling up, be aware of what is upstream. Are you in an area with old mines? Farm or grazing land? A popular hiking trail that has a lot of switchbacks crossing over the same creek many times? Try to get as high/close to the origin source as possible so the water has less time to pick up contamination at the surface. Some of the best-tasting water we have found has come straight out of the side of a mountain—ground-filtered spring water. If you are filling from snowmelt, be aware of pink/watermelon-colored snow (which contains an algae that is toxic to people) and dirty snow.

We discussed water treatment options in more depth in Chapter 6, but I want to add here that if you are filling from a particularly silty or dirty area, you can use your bandanna as a primary filter so your actual water filter doesn't completely clog. If you chemically treat your water rather than filter, then the bandanna also works to keep some of the grit out of your mouth. You can also let really dirty water settle in a vessel before filtering it.

FOOD

In Chapter 2, we discussed food planning and how to calculate how much to bring on the trip. In this section, however, we are taking the food discussion a step further. Let's examine what we typically consume throughout our day, dividing it up break by break.

Breakfast

For breakfast, we aim for something that can be made quickly and consumed fast, so we can get hiking. This usually means a no-cook meal. Mornings can be chilly, so getting out on the trail and moving is key for warming up the body. Another reason we don't cook at breakfast is to reduce the amount of fuel that we need to carry. Last but definitely not least, not having to do dishes in the morning is also pretty great.

Some like a steaming hot cup of coffee in the morning. If that's you, you'll need to carry instant coffee or grounds as well as a vessel to drink from. There are also teabag-style coffee options available. As for filters, either disposable or reusable will do the trick. There are a number of different reusable ones for purchase that come with a contraption that is suspended above your mug. For shorter trips, disposable filters are the lighter-weight option. Or you could make your own coffee teabag by wrapping a portion of grounds in a filter and tying it at the top with dental floss. It won't be as delicious as home brew, but it is lightweight.

In our family, we skip the coffee and focus on calorically dense breakfast shakes made of quick oats, protein powder, dry

Kaleo and Rae chatting over their breakfast shakes on the Colorado Trail.

milk, dehydrated super greens, and a powdered, instant drink pack. Our son loves this shake recipe, but our daughter isn't as big of a fan. We've tried other quick breakfast options for her, including oatmeal, granola, chocolate-coconut hummus and tortillas or crackers, but she always ends up going back to the shakes for quickness and ease of consumption.

Lunch

Out on the trail, we don't usually eat a traditional lunch. We simply eat more snacks. We plan for four snacks each day (eaten during

Breakfast Shakes

Our go-to breakfast shakes meet our morning-meal criteria: quick to assemble, easy to consume, and don't create dishes or mess. They are also calorically dense, about 400 calories for the kids and 600 calories for adults. Here is our recipe, but feel free to get creative based on your family's tastes and appetite.

———

Ground quick oats: ½ cup for kids, ¾ cup for adults

Protein powder: 1 scoop for kids, 2 scoops for adults

Dry milk: 2 tablespoons for kids, ¼ cup for adults

Dehydrated super greens, such as Garden of Life's Raw Organic Perfect Food Green Superfood Original Powder (optional): ¾ tablespoon for kids, 1 tablespoon for adults

Powdered, instant drink mix, such as Carnation Breakfast: 1 package per bottle

———

1. At home, mix dry ingredients together and package in individual bags labeled "A" for adult and "K" for kid (due to different portion sizes).

2. On the trail, in the morning, pour the mix into a bottle that is half filled with water, put the lid on, shake well, and chug.

break stops). When it's time to take a break, we pull out the snack bags, filled with all sorts of foods, and pass them around and munch as we see fit. Dave and I do urge the kids to eat some of the more necessary items (for example, calorically dense and fatty nuts or trail mix need to be eaten along with all the yummy crackers and chips).

We also pack some bars, both homemade (warning: they tend to crumble) and store-bought. It is easy to get tired of the same snacks, so make sure you pack a variety. As discussed in Chapter 2, some fresh fruits and vegetables hold up decently on a backpacking trip, as well as some cheeses.

We dehydrate hummus and rehydrate it for an afternoon snack. Salami, jerky, tuna packets, and other dried or preserved

---

PRO TIP

SOME FRUITS AND VEGGIES travel better than others, and they don't need refrigeration. Eat them on their own or add them to your meals: apples, oranges, carrots, avocado (amazing with dill-flavored crackers), broccoli, cauliflower, cucumber, green beans, snap peas, bell peppers and sweet peppers, onion, and garlic. You can wash them before your trip, and they'll be ready to go! We always loaded our food bags last to avoid squashing them too badly, even though for best weight distribution it makes sense to have the heavy stuff in the center of your pack and close to your back. We also liked them near the top since we pulled them out the most frequently. Remember to pack out any food scraps.

meats are protein-packed trail foods. Avoid chocolate-covered (or yogurt-covered) items in the heat, as these tend to melt and become a big mess.

Having a big bag of tortilla chips or some other treat that the kids don't get at home can be a motivator and a fun bit of excitement to look forward to earning, especially if you've been out on the trail a few days. We have also packed little plastic cups of peanut butter and Nutella to spread on tortillas and roll up to eat. Peanut butter pretzels are also awesome.

If you're hiking in warm temperatures, saltier snacks help to replenish some of the salts you lose to sweat. Get creative! And change it up often so you don't get too sick of it. Put some high-quality stuff in a separate area for later in the trip when the kids are dragging and you need to get them excited again (fruit leathers are excellent treats).

Dinner

Dinner is typically the one meal a day when we pull out the stove and cook, and we usually stop for it before we are done hiking for the day. When the kids start getting hungry any time after 4:00 p.m. or so, we usually announce, "OK, let's look for a good dinner spot!" This lets the kids know that we've heard their complaints and are actively looking to rectify the situation, but at the same time, it lets us get some additional distance in until we're ready to actually stop for dinner. Conversations go something like this:

"How's this spot?" "I dunno, looks kinda slopey."
"How's this spot?" "Hmmm, too many bushes."
"How's this spot?" "Not enough shade."

And so it goes as we continue down the trail, chatting about options and searching for a spot that's *juuuussst* right. Sometimes these exchanges are legitimate reasons, other times we're just stalling and getting them to go a bit farther.

When we find the perfect spot, we all shuck our packs to the ground, and Dave and I usually stretch or sit. The kids will find a miraculous cure for their exhaustion and scramble off to find rocks or water or dirt to play with.

We've found some incredible places to cook meals, including one where we were set up on a sandbar in the middle of a creek surrounded by towering peaks. We've also set up pretty much right on the trail in low-use, overgrown areas. If it's windy, try to find someplace that offers some shelter from the wind. Also, be sure to clear out any dry leaves or brush from the area where you'll be using your stove.

Dave and I will get out the bag holding the meal that one of the kids has picked (we alternate nights, with each kid choosing dinner every other night) and set up the kitchen. He cooks, we chat and relax. I might journal. When the kids were younger, I'd be supervising them to make sure they didn't fall off the rock mountain or into the river.

We have found it easiest to cook in one big pot rather than in multiple smaller ones. It minimizes cleanup and expedites cook

Dave getting dinner going on a sandbar in the middle of a creek in the Flat Tops Wilderness, Colorado.

times. No one has to wait for their meal to be cooked while others are eating. There are fewer things to misplace or forget, and with our system, the stove, spoons, and cook kit fit nicely into the pot for ease of packing.

When the meal has cooked, we let it cool then call the kids over. Everyone grabs their spoon and moves to a quadrant of the pot. For us, it works best to take turns taking a bite, going in a clockwise fashion so there is no arguing over someone getting more or less. When the kids get full, they clean off their spoons by licking them thoroughly and putting them down somewhere *not* in the dirt (we have to stress this last bit a lot). Dave and I finish whatever is left.

Pro Tip: Super-Easy Pot Cleaning

Dave learned a pot-cleaning technique at Scout camp that he uses to this day. Start by scraping out and eating as much food as you can with your spoon. Then add a little water and use your spoon and/or your finger to clean the sides and bottom of the pot. Now here's the fun part: Gulp down the liquid and the remaining food bits. It includes both valuable water and calories! If you just can't handle this (and I admit, it is not for the faint of heart), then spread the remaining liquid far from a water source or your sleeping area using the arc-spray technique. No need for soap. Let the pot drain upside down while you pack up the stove and other food-related items. For stubborn, stuck-on spots, scrub with a pinecone or something similarly abrasive and some water, then do a final rinse.

You'll find a huge variety of backpacking recipes on websites and in magazine and books already out there, so I won't take up space discussing those here. Just remember, the key with dinner is making it warm and tasty—it doesn't need to be fancy and shouldn't be complicated. Simple packaged ramen makes a satisfying and super-easy dinner.

THE KITCHEN

Our kitchen setup has expanded over the years from a tiny alcohol stove (a transformed soda can with holes out the sides for flames) to our old multifuel stove. We discussed stove and fuel options in Chapter 6, but what about all the other equipment? Since we worked to do all the meal planning and prep before heading out on the trail (premixing ingredients into single-bag servings), we know what tools we will need for dinners. This way we can keep it simple, always aware that we'll be carrying it all on our backs.

The most important item is a single, large, titanium pot. Ours has a lid with handles that can also be used as a pan. In addition, we carry a lighter, a little cup with measuring lines on it (a Nalgene with ounces marked on the side will also do), and four hard-plastic spoons saved from a local Froyo shop. If you think about it, you can eat pretty much every kind of backpacking meal with a spoon (especially if you remember to break up any noodles you plan to cook ahead of time). Finally, be sure to bring (and use!) any windscreens that come with your stove to increase the efficiency of your stove.

Treat on the Trail

Unsweetened, dried mango is tough and chewy, in the best way! Its sweetness makes for a great snack or a satisfying end to any meal, and the fact that it takes so long to eat makes it the equivalent of backcountry gum in my opinion. To make the package last longer, cut large pieces into smaller strips. The strips will keep younger kids' hands less sticky if they can just pop them into their mouths whole.

11

Games and Rewards

THIS IS THE GOLDEN CHAPTER. Maybe you have backpacked before kids, so you come to this book with a pretty good understanding of what goes into planning a trip, the gear you prefer, and so forth—you just need to understand the best ways to adapt that to kids. The biggest change, and unknown, is what the heck you're going to do with your kids for all those hours of the day when you're walking! And oh my goodness, there are *a lot* of hours in the day!

DELIGHTS, DISTRACTIONS, AND DIVERSIONS ON THE TRAIL

I don't know what your kids are like, but mine were definitely not introspective little souls who preferred to ponder the meaning of life in silence as we trip-tropped along the trail. No. There was no silence to be had once we started hiking with our kids. And we

Rae and Kaleo winding down by making up tales with Story Cubes.

had to quickly become versed in all the ways to keep them occupied and somewhat complacent, if not happy, so we could keep doing what we loved, which was hiking.

We figured it was win-win. The kids get all our attention, and we get to be outdoors. What we didn't fully comprehend was how exhausting it can be to occupy a little human for that long for days on end while also dealing with your own physical and mental needs. Without any breaks!

Here I've collected some of our family's favorite ways to pass the time in nature. These are trail-tested and kid-approved. We've played them hiking, on breaks, waiting for dinner to cook, and as ways to calm down at bedtime.

Give them a try, or springboard off these ideas to create your own. There are also websites and books with loads of ideas to try. Figuring out what everyone enjoys is part of the fun!

DIY Stories and Songs

My husband and I tell a lot of stories. Big, long, fantastic stories that go on for hours and never really truly have a point or completion until we get to a spot to stop for dinner (or lunch or breaks).

My husband is amazing at this. His creative side comes out full force, and the kids aren't the only ones who are fascinated. Many times, I find myself drawn in to see where exactly he's taking this particular monster or where he's thinking of launching that particular coconut. He creates songs that the kids bring up long after we've left the trail: "Burrito in My Belly" and "I've Got Dirt at the Bottom of My Water Bottle" are just two of his memorable hits.

Besides being great entertainment, his leading the charge on story time lets me go on ahead or fall behind just a bit, just enough to get lost in my own thoughts and to have a moment of peace. It's beautiful. And when his story comes to an end and after we have our food break, I'm up to bat, and he gets a break to sink into himself.

Retelling Classics

I have a harder time coming up with brand-new stories on the spot like my husband can. I learned that my strength is in recalling movie and book plots and editing them so they're suitable for our kids' ears. Leaning on the writings of others, I keep my kids

> **PRO TIP**
>
> **BRUSH UP** on your movies and literature before heading out on your next backpacking trip, so you'll be fully prepared with stories that will engage your kids.

fully entertained for hours. We had them quoting classics from movies, such as *Monty Python and the Holy Grail*, *Beetlejuice*, and *The Princess Bride,* long before they were allowed to actually see the films. We recently watched *Beetlejuice* with them for the first time, they thought it was hysterical, and now they understand those quotes so much better!

Design Your Own . . .

Many kids love the idea of designing their own things. Mine have spent hours verbally designing dream homes, RVs, and tree-houses as we walk down the trail. We ask leading questions—Does your treehouse have an ice cream bar? Does your house have an indoor pool with an aquarium of sharks on the other side? Does your RV have the ability to shrink down to pocket-size so you can carry it with you while you're on the trail then drive again once you're in town?—and their imaginations run wild. They've created entire worlds that include mosquitoes as big as trees and lava-squirting mushrooms that you have to swing past on vines into treehouses under the ground.

If your kids are more tech inclined, they could design their own video games. Encourage them to think about all the different levels and challenges, the bosses and bad guys, the racetracks, the rewards or penalties. The beauty of these imagination games is that by simply actively (or even passively) listening and inserting a few well-timed prompts or questions, you can rest your mouth and brain and stay quiet as the kids build their own stories.

Many Questions

This game takes the old standard Twenty Questions and twists it slightly: In our version, we don't keep track of how many questions we all ask. For us, the game rotates among players as to who gets to pick the item in question. Once the item is chosen, the questions run the gamut, as you try to narrow things down:

Is it man-made? Can you buy it in a store? Is it with us on this trip? Does anyone we know own it? Is it bigger/smaller than me? Is it found in . . . ? Is it made of plastic/metal/fabric/wood? Is it natural? Is it a plant/tree/flower/fungus? Is it a mammal? Reptile? Insect? Can we see it?

(As for that last question, yes, this did come into play when our son decided to start using adjectives as the thing we were supposed to guess. So you might want to set the ground rule that it has to be a real, tangible, visible, noun-type thing. It can't just be the word "awesome." Stinker.)

Round-Robin Stories

Round-robin storytelling does require you to pay a good bit of attention, but just to the person in front of you in the story line. Once our kids were in preschool, their imaginations started working overtime. This game let us harness that creativity and spin it into entertainment. Here's how it works: Someone comes up with a story and starts telling it for however long they wish. When the storyteller stops, he or she then passes to the next person in your group who continues the story however they see fit, and so on and so forth throughout the group.

You never know where these stories will take you. One of our stories started innocently enough with a moose, until we learned that he had five antlers and breathed fire and had a laser beam coming out of his backside and was best friends with a bunny who would get so mad when people mispronounced his last name—"It's Guden*stein*! *Not* Guden*steen*!!!"—that he would eat them. It made the moose sad when the bunny ate the man who served them tea in the tea house, so the moose decided they couldn't be friends any more. Somehow the moose ended up getting captured and sold to a circus. There was a train and Steve Irwin involved, and it's all very complicated and completely wild, but it was also amazing and exactly how you want these stories to go. Have fun with it!

Songs with the Word . . .

This fun singing game can be tailored to your kid's ages and abilities. At 10 and 12, our kids have a huge database of song lyrics in their heads, but even when they were littles, they had some song knowledge, so if you said, "Sing a song with the word 'boat' in it," they could sing "Row, row, row your boat," and you could all sing the song together.

As kids get older, it turns into a back-and-forth competition. So if the word is "boat," and one person sings the line "Row, row, row your boat," then the next person has to think of a different song with boat in it, such as "Sailing down the coast in my little rowboat, woah oh" (Jimmy Cliff, "Brown Eyes"). The next person might come up with the line, "Rock the boat, don't rock the boat baby" (Hues Corporation, "Rock the Boat"), and another might sing, "Sit down, you're rocking the boat!" (Guys and Dolls, "Sit Down You're Rocking the Boat"), and so on and so forth until you can't come up with any other songs.

You can decide how strict you'll be on lyric judgments (we say you need to know four or five words of the song in order for it to count; you can't just say "boat" and hum the tune). If you want a game that has a "winner," then it can be the last person who is able to think of a song with a particular word. The winner gets to pick the next word.

Two Truths and a Lie

This can be tricky in a family, as you know a lot about each other already, but it can also be a fun way to learn about your kids likes and dislikes (and for them to learn about yours!). For example, your younger kid might say, "My favorite color is purple, my favorite fruit is grapes, and the place I most want to visit is France," and from this list, the rest of you have to guess which of those three statements is a lie. If the kids have trouble coming up with things, you can take the lead and give them categories, such as favorite songs, seasons, holidays, places they want to go, school subjects, trees, or animals. It is interesting to hear what your older kids come up with. And you'll also see what good little liars they can be!

Would You Rather

Our kids are so obsessed with this game that they play it at home too. Topics can range from gross to wonderful, logical to fantastical—the sky is the limit. This game is played when someone comes up with a question that starts with "Would you rather . . ." and offers two alternative scenarios. It can be anything from eating different items, traveling to different places, having different pets, or anything else. Everyone can take turns answering. It is fun to see if there is a general consensus or if folks have differing opinions on what they'd rather do. There aren't any winners in this game; it is just a fun way to pass the time. Here are a few ideas to get you started.

- ▸ Would you rather have to eat a worm or a booger? (Guaranteed one of the kids will fess up to already eating a booger. Or a worm.)
- ▸ Would you rather have a magical unicorn or an otter for a pet?
- ▸ Would you rather live in space or under the water?
- ▸ Would you rather have wings and be able to fly or gills and be able to stay underwater?
- ▸ Would you rather have pink hair or purple hair?
- ▸ Would you rather be rich but annoying or poor but nice?

Mystery Box

Mystery Box is basically a homemade trivia game. The kids ask for a Mystery Box, and we ask them for different facts of varying degrees of difficulty. Usually, the question-asker picks the topic to ask each person individually in order to tailor it to their abilities and interests (which makes it great for all age ranges), but sometimes the kids will ask just a general question for anyone to answer. Bonus: You can make this game educational without them even realizing it! They ask us questions too, and it is funny hearing what they come up with. Mix in some pop trivia now and again to keep them coming back for more. Here are some examples of questions that might be in the Mystery Box:

Toddler to early elementary:

- ▸ Name three types of cereal.
- ▸ Name five colors.
- ▸ Name seven animals.

Later elementary to middle school:

- ▸ Name ten states or capitals.
- ▸ Name eight of your favorite songs.
- ▸ Name five animals that live in our state.

High school:

- ▸ Name seven lakes in the world.
- ▸ Name 10 elements from the periodic table.
- ▸ Name 15 bones in the body.

Any age:

- ▸ Name five movies.
- ▸ Name eight books.
- ▸ Name 10 characters from shows, books, or movies.

Story Cubes

Story Cubes are a set of nine dicelike cubes that have different images on each side. They come in a small traveling pouch, and you can wash them off if they get dirty. The idea is that you roll the dice and come up with a story using the images that land face up. Instructions say this game is for ages 8 and up, but my son has been spinning absolute nonsensical tales much longer than that, so as long as you can deal with some real doozies, kids can play this game way younger. It is easy enough that the kids can play on their own while dinner is being made or while grown-ups are doing other chores.

Dice

Dice games are fun if your kids get tired of Story Cubes or if you just want to mix it up a bit. Run a web search on instructions for games like Liar's Dice or Farkle. They involve varying numbers of dice, which of course is added weight in your pack, so determine if you have the wiggle room to carry this particular entertainment option.

Who Thinks

This game is for slightly older children who understand the concept of estimating and guesstimating. In this game, you alternate whose turn it is every round. So in a four-person family, if it's Daddy's turn first, he might say, "(Insert child A's name) thinks that there are this many countries in Africa." Without telling anyone their guess, child A will think of how many countries there are in Africa and hold that number in their head (or write it down if they have paper and a pencil). Every person except child A takes turns guessing what the child thinks. Mom might say, "I guess child A thinks there are 30 countries." Child B might say, "I guess child A thinks there are three countries." Dad might say, "I guess child A thinks there are 150 countries in Africa." Then child A says, "I thought there were five countries!" Child B was closest! So child B wins and goes next, saying, "(Insert family member's name) thinks there are X number of Y in Z," and so on and so forth (number of cheerios in a box of cereal, number of forks in the kitchen drawer back home, number of students in their school, number of animals in the zoo, number of miles to the moon, and so on). Whoever is closest wins and gets to go next. The brilliance of this game is that you don't actually need to know the answers to anything. It is completely determined by what that person *thinks* is the right answer.

Reward Systems

Reward systems (OK, bribery) can be very effective. On our backpacking trips, we have created a reward system that for every mile the kids hike in a day, they get a jelly bean (you can use M&M's or whatever they enjoy, just make sure it's small, so you aren't carrying too much extra weight at the beginning of your trip). When they started increasing their daily mileages, we offered them two jelly beans for every mile that was in the double digits. So if we hiked 13 miles in a day (an average day on the Tahoe Rim Trail), then they would get nine jelly beans for miles 1 through 9, plus eight jelly beans for miles 10 through 13, so 17 jelly beans total. It can add up fast. The kids loved sitting down and adding up the mileage, then calculating their winnings. It was just enough to keep them motivated.

You can divvy up the weight by making a bag of rewards for each kid ahead of time and letting them carry it themselves in their packs. That means less weight in your bag, and the kids definitely don't mind carrying candy! (Just remember to pull them out of the packs and put them in the bear bags at night if you're in bear country.)

Jelly beans also make for great entertainment for guessing the flavors and trading. Sometimes we split up the morning and afternoon miles, so the kids can have some of their jelly beans at lunch as a "reward" for miles hiked in the morning.

On the flip side, they can also *lose* jelly beans if they don't cooperate in the tent at night. If they have a tough time calming and quieting at night, we remove jelly beans for the next day. This method usually got them to go to bed faster and also kept us from running out of jelly beans on one particular trip where they had gotten much faster than we had anticipated! Moral of that story: bring more rewards than you initially think necessary.

We often let the kids pick out one king-size candy bar per day for our backpacking trips. Sometimes we may adjust that depending on the length and difficulty of the trip. The kids get to pick out what kinds they want, and the parents get to deal with the side glances from the cashier when you bring twenty candy bars to be rung up at the grocery store for four people on a five-day trip.

Counting out jelly beans after a day of hiking on the Tahoe Rim Trail, Nevada. Photo by David Heinrich

PART 5

ANTICIPATE

12

Overcoming Obstacles

LIONS AND MOSQUITOES AND BEARS, OH MY! There are so many creatures out in nature. Add the fact that one can never be too sure exactly what the weather is going to do, and you have a combination that makes many would-be backpackers hesitant to leave the familiar and strike out into the unknown. Especially with kids in tow. The aim of this chapter is to ease that concern by putting some of the control back in your hands, as much as is possible. In this section, I'll outline techniques to help you prepare for some of the encounters or elements you may encounter, and in doing so, hopefully make your experience more, well, *bear*able!

ANIMALS

The most reassuring thing for you to know is this: animals in the woods don't typically want to eat people. Humans are not their normal food source, and for the most part, they have learned to stay away. Even so, there are precautions that you and your family can and should take when entering the backcountry in order to stay animal-safe.

The most important rule of thumb is to give any wild animal you come across plenty of space. Surprising an animal is a surefire way to kick off their fight-or-flight reflex. Avoid this potentially negative interaction by putting bear bells on packs or shoes and by keeping up a steady stream of chatter, singing, or game-playing. Honestly, when we are hiking with our kids, we rarely see wildlife because we are making so much noise on the trail! And if we are in a known bear/lion/moose area, we will purposely clap or call out "Hey, Bear!" every now and again.

A big concern when it comes to animals is accidently ending up near or—even worse—*between* a mom and her babies. There is a reason that women are cool with identifying as a "mama bear" if someone messes with their kid. Mama bears—and other animal mothers—are fierce when it comes to protecting family. If you ever see a cub, it is pretty much guaranteed that mama is somewhere nearby, and you should get out of there. Keep moving. Keep making noise. Definitely don't approach the cute, cuddly-looking creature.

Food smells can lure unwanted guests to your camp. For breakfast and snacks/lunch, it usually isn't an issue because we pack up and walk away from the smells after we're done eating. At dinner, we've learned to prevent issues by stopping to cook and eat prior to where we'll be setting up camp for the night. We do dinner, clean the dishes, brush our teeth, and then hike on at least another half mile to get away from the dinner smells before setting up camp for the night. A bear bag helps eliminate odors that are attractive to bears and other critters (see "Bear Bags and Bear Canisters," p. 152).

Bears

When hiking in bear country, carry bear spray and know how to use it. According to the National Park Service, if you encounter a bear, you should make yourself big, stay calm, and talk in a commanding, low voice. Pick up small children. Don't allow the bear access to your food and don't drop your pack (your pack can be protection if the bear attacks). Don't run or climb trees. Leave the area by taking a detour if possible. Clack your trekking poles together if you have them.

Black bears will typically flee (unless you've come between a mom and her cubs). If, however, a black bear approaches, stand and face the bear. Neither run away nor go toward it. Make yourself look big and make a lot of noise, banging pots and pans if possible. If it charges or attacks, do *not* play dead. They may be bluffing, in which case you should stand your ground until they go away. If they do attack, fight back using any object available. Focus your kicks and hits on the bear's face and muzzle.

Rules for a grizzly attack are the opposite for black bears. Yellowstone National Park says that if a grizzly is surprised, it will clack its teeth, stick out its lips, huff, woof, or slap the ground with its paws to show you it is nervous. You should calmly and quietly back away slowly while getting your bear spray ready. If

Bear Bags and Bear Canisters

We bring along bear bags or bear canisters for food and other odorous items (such as toothpaste and sunblock, which also go in the bear bag at night). Bear canisters are solid plastic food-storage containers that bears cannot open (they are heavier and bulkier than bear bags). Bear bags are reusable Kevlar bags that have removable metal cylinders, which provide increased food protection. Both types of containers have the benefit of not needing to be hung in a tree at camp. For bear bags, you simply tie off the opening at the top and then use a square knot to tie the bag directly to a tree or branch. We once had a bear take our bag

Dave hanging our bear bags in Yellowstone National Park.

(we hadn't tied it as well as we should have), so we had to go on a treasure hunt for it the next day. We found the bag about 50 feet from our tents, with teeth indents and slobber evident on the exterior, our food a bit crushed, but all of it safe and inaccessible. The bear didn't get in, and the bag did what it was supposed to do; the bear lost interest and left it alone. The National Park Service recommends leaving bear bags and canisters 100 yards downwind from your tent and away from cliffs and water sources.

We are careful to put all toiletries and snacks into these bags, along with any food. It's easy for kids to forget wrappers or small snacks in their packs at night, so we make a habit of going through everything before bed and putting all smelly items into the bear bags.

Some areas require bear canisters (they don't allow bear bags) or provide bear boxes that you're expected to use. We've also been to places with food-bag hanging systems. Be sure to research the rules and regulations and comply, in order to keep both you and the wildlife safe. We always bring rope to hang our food if necessary. Bear canisters can be rented from some outdoor supply stores or parks.

it charges you and does not veer off in a bluff charge, spray it with bear spray when it is 40 feet away or closer, then at the last second before contact, fall to the ground facedown and play dead with your hands behind your head covering your neck, using your pack as protection for your back. Spread your legs to make it harder for the bear to turn you over. Stay still and hope the bear leaves.

If a grizzly attack isn't due to surprise and there are none of those nervous signs—instead the bear is curious or preda-tory, approaching you with ears up and head up—fight back with everything you have by hitting the bear in the face.

If any bear attacks you in your tent, fight back.

We've seen numerous black bears on our trips, and even had one come toward our camp that we deterred by getting big (arms over our head) and asking it loudly and firmly to go away. Our kids stayed behind us and watched as the bear veered off up the mountain. They followed our lead and stayed calm, but we all had a lively discussion about how cool that was when we started hiking again. My husband and I both had bear spray on our hip belts when we backpacked in Yellowstone and the Grand Tetons, but we never saw a bear (other than one that had been hit by a car and killed, sadly).

Mountain Lions

Mountain lions, while big and scary with their claws and sharp teeth, rarely attack people unless they are surprised, protecting their young, or protecting a recent animal kill. If you are hiking in mountain lion territory, keep your kids close to you. Don't let them lag behind the group, nor scurry ahead, which kids some-times love to do. Always keep them in sight. According to the National Park Service, if you see a mountain lion, stay calm, hold your ground, or walk away slowly while facing the lion and stand-ing upright. Be big. Don't squat or bend over, even to pick up your kid (it makes you look like prey). Open up your jacket to look bigger if you're wearing one. Wave your arms slowly and speak in a calm, loud voice. Don't be high-pitched or scream. If the lion moves in your direction, try to be as intimidating as possible and throw stones while minimizing crouching or bending. I know, easier said than done, but your kids can pass sticks and rocks to you while staying right behind you, or you can grab stuff from nearby trees or even throw your water bottles. (Just hold on to one of the water bottles to use as a weapon if things escalate.) Mountain lions try to attack necks, so keep your pack on as a shield if the encounter gets that close. Fight back with anything available to you.

We have been in mountain lion country on almost all our backpacking trips. We have had a few hikers tell us, "Watch out, there's a mountain lion on a rock around this bend," but we have never seen one. We know that they have seen us, but they've never bothered us. We are loud; we talk and sing. Maybe they've decided we aren't worth the effort.

Moose

If you get charged by a moose, the advice is simple: *Run!* Try to put a tree or other object between you and the moose. Moose have very poor eyesight and can be very aggressive. Enjoy these impressive mammals from a distance.

Rodents

Not all animal encounters are of the super-sized kind. In fact, you're far more likely to have a negative rodent encounter than

GIVE WILDLIFE as much space as possible. Animals with their young are especially protective and irritable, so give them even more space. Bells on your pack or lots of talking, clapping, and singing in remote areas helps to give creatures a heads up and time to move away from you. As a general rule, hike with one adult in the front of the group, and another at the rear if possible.

large mammal encounter in the woods. Unfortunately, many rodents in popular areas have become habituated to humans and have come to associate backpackers with food. Their sharp, tiny teeth can chew through packs, stuff sacks, and plastic bags. We once had a rodent chew a hole through a bear-proof Kevlar bag and get a candy bar (this is one reason why bear canisters are considered superior).

Snakes

Snakes live where we like to hike. Be aware of what types of snakes live in the region you're backpacking in. Know some basic information about them, such as if they are venomous or not, as well as treatment options for bites.

Simply being aware of your surroundings when hiking can prevent many unfortunate encounters, as some snakes (such as rattlers) have built-in warning systems that they'll use to alert you of their presence, such as a rattle. Other times snakes may slither away from you unnoticed.

According to NOLS, if someone in your party is bitten, it is important to try to keep them calm and to remove any restrictive clothing or jewelry. Wash the area with soap and water. Wound dressing in your first aid kit could be used to keep the area clean and dry.

Some popular myths surround snake-bite treatment, but many are false. For example, don't apply heat or cold to the area, don't use a tourniquet, and don't try to suck the venom out. Circle or mark the edge of swelling and pain in Sharpie (have it in your first aid kit) and write the time on the ink outline to track progress of inflammation and update the line every 15 to 30 minutes.

Try to remember what the snake looked like or snap a picture without getting too close. Keep the wound at the elevation of the heart or lower. Call for help and evacuate. The victim should immediately be evacuated to the nearest medical facility that has anti-venom available. This is the only effective treatment for snakebites (most urgent care centers do have anti-venom). Walk the victim out slowly and calmly if they are able to on their own to a trailhead or road and get medical help (have someone carry the victim's pack). If not, contact EMS or search and rescue for evacuation.

Medical attention should be sought regardless of whether you think the snake is poisonous or non-poisonous.

BUGS

Bugs are inevitable but can sometimes be largely avoided simply by choosing to go into the backcountry at particular times of the year. Before your trip, make sure to research the general timing for things like fly hatches and mosquito peak times in the area. Early fall, when nighttime temperatures begin to dip but daytimes are still warm, can be a great way to avoid most bug issues.

Mosquitoes

Mosquito season in certain areas can really, well, suck! Whether you need to take precautionary measures largely depends on how many mosquitoes there are and how potent your personal body chemistry is. My daughter always gets attacked more than any of us, poor girl.

We carry different levels of protection depending on the severity of the situation. We try to avoid putting DEET or other chemicals on our entire bodies for multiple days in a row, especially if we won't have a way to clean it off before going into our sleeping bags for the night.

Clothing offers a chemical-free way to get protection, depending on the gear. We have found that our nylon wind pants and wind jackets are mosquito-proof, while Lycra and cotton leggings are usually not.

The MVP piece of gear in our packs recently has been a mosquito head net. It is amazing for keeping your sanity in mosquito country because it keeps the little guys from hovering right around your ears. We passed many agitated hikers that were continually fanning their faces with their hats or batting around their heads with their hands trying to keep the blood suckers away.

Mosquito head nets are cheap and super lightweight. If you have a hat with a brim all the way around it, such as a bucket-style or fisherman's hat, the brim will keep the net away from your face and neck. We hike with baseball caps a lot, and the netting rests on the backs of our necks if we aren't careful, leaving them vulnerable to bites. Tucking a bandanna under your hat and having it hang down the back of your neck and over the ears usually pushes the net far enough away to keep mosquitoes from reaching skin.

Plant-based repellent is another option—look for one that has earned the CDC stamp of effectiveness. We tend to carry a small container with us for use on hands or other body parts when it is too hot to wear wind jackets or if it is our last day on the trail and we know we'll be able to wash it off that night.

Other Flying Pests

Mosquitoes are not the only irritants you may run into. Black flies, horse and deer flies, gnats, no-see-ums, and other flying insects can all put a damper on your backcountry experience. Treatment for these is similar to that for mosquitoes. If you choose to use a spray, be sure to read the label to see what it protects against. A finer mesh will keep no-see-ums out of your head net and tent, and a thin nylon shell can prevent many of these pests from getting to your skin.

Cranky Kids

One of the biggest obstacles—and one you'll likely encounter on every backpacking trip—is crankiness. Yes, we have that wonderful section about keeping kids entertained on the trail, but the truth is, all the fun in the world can't keep crankiness at bay forever. The good news is that crabbiness is usually caused by one of four things: thirst/dehydration, hunger, boredom, or exhaustion.

Thirst and hunger are the most common causes and should be addressed first. I discussed both in Chapter 10. Boredom can hopefully be alleviated with a variety of creative games (see Chapter 11). Exhaustion is harder to read. It could be a sign that you've bitten off more than you can chew, which means you might need to reevaluate daily mileage or pacing goals. Or it might simply be that your kids need a rest break before going again. Give them a break, get them hydrated and fed, and then reassess.

Ticks

Ticks are a menace of a different sort. When we took a trip to tick country, we treated our pants, socks, wind jackets, and shirts with permethrin, and my son still got a tick in his arm (he had removed his jacket for a few hours, and that was all it took). Sometimes you have to weigh your options against the bugs in a particular area and use chemicals if you feel it is worth it for what you're walking through. There are plant-based tick repellants that have also earned the CDC stamp of effectiveness.

Regardless of what method you use, it's important to do tick checks multiple times per day when in tick country. If you find a tick that has bitten someone in your group, remove it as soon as possible using pointy tweezers. Do not yank it out, as its mouth could remain. Slide the tweezers between the skin and the tick's mouth. Gently pull the tick straight up and away from the skin and try to keep it all in one piece. It may take a few tries. Wash the area with antiseptic or soap and water.

If a tick is removed within twenty-four hours of it getting engorged in the skin, Lyme disease transmission is less likely. For extra assurance, you can seal the tick in a bag and send it to a lab to be tested for Lyme and other diseases (Google "where to send ticks for testing"). Monitor the bitten person for swelling, pain, stiffness, rashes, fainting, fever, or chills for thirty days. See a doctor if any symptoms are experienced.

WEATHER

Always check the forecast before you head out on a trip in order to plan what to expect and how to keep everyone comfortable (knowing that meteorologists aren't perfect). Weather can be fickle, but as long as you're prepared, you can get through a lot more than you think out in the wild. We've already discussed various weather gear to pack (see Chapter 14). Now let's dive into what you can actually do to stay safe and keep everyone's spirits up when different weather phenomena are encountered on the trail.

Rain

Rain is sneaky. It may not seem like a big deal at first, but it is important to take it seriously to avoid slipping or getting too cold. If it looks like there will be a lot of rain in the forecast, think about if your family will still enjoy the outing or if you should reschedule (take a rain check, as it were).

If you're caught in rain, assure the kids that no one ever melted in the rain, but at the same time make sure to keep them warm. Encourage them to put on a warm hat to prevent heat loss. Make sure fingers and extremities are protected. Umbrellas are excellent for keeping the rain away from your core when hiking, allowing you to adjust your layers (you can continue to hike in a short-sleeve shirt if you're warm or in warmer layers if it is cooler—you aren't limited to wearing your rain jacket).

If it is the middle of the day and you're able to keep hiking, go for it. Movement will keep bodies warmer than sitting still. Shoes will get wet, but that's okay—they'll dry eventually. If it is the end of the day and you're ready to set up camp, have the kids continue to move while you set up tents so they are able to keep warm. Put on the other pair of dry socks you're carrying, and hang wet stuff outside under your tent vestibule. Take extra care to protect down gear from moisture as it loses its ability to insulate when wet.

Be aware that setting up or breaking down a tent in the rain can be a real test of flexibility and maneuvering to keep the sleeping bags dry. To add insult to injury, if you have a single-wall tent, the inside walls may become covered in condensation that can lead to your gear (including down sleeping bags) getting wet from inside. Hopefully you'll have some sunny, warm weather later in the day and can dry out your gear.

Beware of what I call the rain "domino effect." Rain for days on end, especially in colder temperatures, means it will be more and more difficult to keep your gear dry and your body heat up. Extremities, like your feet and hands, can get miserably and dangerously cold when your gloves or shoes are wet for days. Which means it may become harder to have fun with kids. The good news is that usually such prolonged weather systems are reported in advance, so again, check the weather app or news before you head out on your trip.

Thunderstorms and Lightning

Thunder and lightning storms are not uncommon during peak backpacking season. Always check the forecast before your trip. Due to the danger of lightning, it is important to be off mountains or exposed passes by noon if possible, so be sure to take this into account as you plan your route and number of daily miles.

If you are hiking with young kids who might not be able to move quickly to safety if a storm comes in, stick to lower elevations below tree line when plotting out your trip. If you are caught in a storm, look for a nearby valley or depression to wait it out, but avoid pooling water as electricity travels quickly through it. If you do get stuck in a lightning storm with nowhere to go, prepare to hunker down. Make sure metal trekking poles and framed packs are at least 100 feet away from you. If your kids are old enough, spread the family out so that you are 100 feet away from each other. Instruct your kids to crouch low on the balls of their feet, with feet together, head low and ears covered until danger has passed. Don't lie on the ground. To learn more about lightning safety, seek out the wide variety of resources and advice that can be found online, including at NOAA.gov.

Wind

Hiking in high-wind areas can be difficult both physically and mentally. It can be loud, it can make walking more strenuous, and it can be dangerous when in exposed areas. Nylon wind jackets and pants go a long way toward keeping your body temperature regulated in high winds. Finding shelter behind trees or rocks is great for taking breaks or cooking food. We've used our umbrellas as wind breaks for the stove to make it easier to light and maintain the flame.

Avoid camping on ridges or saddles in windy areas, as these tend to be the windiest. Trees can provide a buffer, but be sure not to set up near dead trees as they could fall. Be aware of how you set your tent up in windy areas. Keep tie-downs very taught. If your tent is made of sil nylon (a typical fabric for lightweight backpacking tents), you may need to reset your stakes after your tent has been pitched for twenty to thirty minutes as the material can stretch a bit after initial setup. Be extra careful with food wrappers in the wind to make sure they make it into your garbage. Never have campfires in windy areas as the sparks can cause forest fires.

Snow

If you're going to be in high country when there is still snow on the ground, do your research. Know generally where the snow line is. Is there still snow in the trees that could make routefinding challenging or travel difficult due to post-holing? Is the snow primarily above tree line? Is it a popular route that will be heavily traveled, and therefore a path will be fairly easy to follow (knowing that in high-melt season, the path could be melted away each day)?

Having a map and some routefinding skills are important when your explorations will take you over snow. Patience is also key. Taking the time to kick steps into snow so the kids can easily make their way is really helpful to get up and over snowdrifts. Trekking poles or sticks can help kids balance over slippery cross-slopes. If they don't have their own, give one of your poles to the kids for their use in crossing a snowfield.

Snow increases your exposure to the sun's rays. Rays are reflected off the snow and can burn parts of your body that may not typically burn (for example, your chin, under your nose, even the roof of your mouth!). Always be sure to apply sun protection or wear protective clothing if you're going to be spending a decent amount of time on snow.

If you are in a safe area (not too steep or rocky) it can be fun to shoe-ski down snowdrifts. It is basically a standing glissade: just bend your knees, put your feet in a classic downhill ski stance, and slide down the snow. I usually let my husband (and his big feet) go first to lay the tracks for the rest of us to follow. Alternately, you can sit on your butt and scoot down in a traditional glissade. Just know that snow can tear pants and tends to go up shorts, and you'll wind up wet. Watch for hazards below—be sure you can stop and have a sufficient runout zone.

On a hike in high country, we'd gone over a pass, and there was a bunch of snow down to where we could clearly see the trail below, maybe a football field away. After weighing the risks, we decided we'd glissade it on our butts. Dave went first, paving the way, standing when he got to the bottom. Rae went next, and she slowed a bit sooner, not quite reaching the trail. Kaleo followed after her, but he stopped even sooner. I went after him, ended up *not* slowing down, and plowed right into him. Together we then slid down into his sister, who was trying to scramble out of the way (we all had our packs on, so it was like bumper cars). The three of us ended in one big heap, laughing our heads off while Dave got a video of it. The kids were shocked that their mother ran them over since I'm normally the one reminding everyone to be careful!

In snow country, always be aware of cornices. These are large, overhanging waves of wind-swept snow. If you are approaching from the upwind side of a pass, be careful not to walk out onto a cornice that could collapse. If you are approaching from the downwind side, make a plan to go around (not under) cornices if possible.

Our backpacking trip in the Paria Canyon got cut short when we spoke to the local rangers who let us know the freezing water was chest-deep in one branch of the canyon. We stuck to the shallower areas and made our trip an out-and-back rather than a loop. Photo by David Heinrich

WATER CROSSINGS

Water can be tempestuous. And despite best efforts with planning and research, water levels can and do change quickly. If you come to unexpected high water and need to cross it, there are a few strategies you can use. I have explained some here, but for more detailed information, check out the National Park Service river crossing link in the "Helpful Resources" section.

Do your research in advance. Examine where your trip will take you and the potential water crossings. Look for recent trip reports online from other backpackers or hikers. When you are onsite, talk to local rangers, if there are any, to hear updated information on what levels are like.

When you arrive at crossings, reevaluate the situation, based on real-time conditions. Assess the strength, depth, and movement of the water. Toss in a stick and see how quickly it floats downstream. Toss in a rock and see what sound it makes (a shallow plink or a deep ka-thump). Avoid crossing water deeper than knee-height if possible unless there is little to no current. Watch out for submerged logs or other water hazards that could trip you or hold you under. Are you comfortable having your kids cross this water? Safety should be most important. Remember that younger kids' legs are shorter, which puts the water level higher up their bodies. Water that is below your knees may be above theirs.

If you deem that it's safe for you all to cross, here are some tips to keep in mind to keep things dry:

- Place key safety items into watertight stuff sacks or plastic bags in case you fall.
- Line packs with trash-compactor bags, which increases the packs' buoyancy.
- Place any dangling or drying items inside the pack.
- Seal up electronics, toys, and stuffed animals.
- If you're not wearing them, change into wool socks, which will keep feet warm when wet.
- If you are wearing waterproof boots/shoes, consider removing insoles and socks before crossing. (Do *not* cross in bare feet. Unstable footing can mean the difference between safety and injury, or worse.) If your shoes aren't waterproof, they will dry without you taking the step to remove insoles and socks.
- Roll up pants or put on shorts to decrease drag.
- Use hiking poles or stout sticks to maintain balance and test for foot placements.
- Discuss your crossing technique in advance; for example, what order you will cross in or if will you lock elbows or arms.

There are better and worse times to cross waterways, as far as seasons go. Mountain streams are fed from runoff of melting snow. They are lowest in the cooler mornings and highest in the late afternoon. Cross at a straight section of stream through the widest channel or where there are many braided channels instead of just one, in hopes of finding slower, shallower crossing points. I don't usually advocate for going off-trail, but if you need to do so to find a safer crossing point, you can walk up and down the stream.

Be aware of hazards downstream and have a rescue plan. Are there large rocks, trees, or waterfalls downstream? If someone falls, how will you help them before they reach those hazards? If you don't think you can cross safely, be comfortable with turning around if that is what is best for the group. Usually, a crossing this questionable will be large enough to be shown on a map. It is unlikely that you'll run into a "turn-around" scenario with proper preparation (we haven't yet), but if it is a concern, you could plan for this potential outcome by packing enough supplies to backtrack.

As you prepare to enter the water, have everyone unclip their hip belts and sternum straps, so that if anyone falls, they will be able to easily remove their pack if it flips them on their face in the water. As you cross, face upstream and shuffle your feet along the bottom, moving in a slightly downstream direction across the water. Try to keep at least two points of contact with the ground at all times with a trekking pole or stick. Have the stronger person upstream to break the current. Turn back if it becomes questionable. Safety first! When you get across, take time to remove wet shoes and socks, squeeze out excess water and maybe even have a snack break to dry off and celebrate your adventure.

BLOWDOWNS (FALLEN TREES)

When walking in areas where a lot of trees have fallen, take time to look around and assess the canopy above. Have healthy trees fallen, perhaps due to blowdowns or a lightning strike, or are you in an area with mostly dead trees? Dead trees are not only a hassle to navigate around when they have fallen across your trail, but they can also signal that there might be danger from above in the form of falling branches. Be vigilant as you move through the area, especially when winds are high. Areas of recent forest fires can be especially dangerous during high winds.

When it comes to finding your way around fallen trees on the trail, proceed slowly and carefully, remembering that it may be easier for kids to go under rather than over. Have them pass you their pack first, then crawl under (or leave the pack on for protection in case they stand up before being fully cleared). Finally, always make sure that where you're setting up your tent or sitting down for a break is not in danger of falling trees or limbs.

13

Hygiene

TAKING CARE OF PHYSICAL HYGIENE on the trail looks a little different than it does at home. Instead of having access to running water and a drain, various soaps and products, and all the supplies you'd find in your bathroom, you make do with a few carefully selected items that hold you over for a few days (or longer) before you return to civilization. While throwing caution to the wind and letting your family go a little more *au natural* is totally fine (feel free to leave razors and deodorant at home!), there are some basic practices that you'll want to maintain to ensure everyone keeps discomfort, doctors, and dentists away.

KEEPING CLEAN

"Clean" is a relative term when you're backpacking, but by keeping key parts of bodies clean, you'll be able to enjoy hanging out in the backcountry longer. Bandannas or handkerchiefs are the

MVPs of this section. When you are backpacking in an area with water sources, try to stop at one at least once a day for a wash (if it can be near the end of the day, that's a bonus).

Fill your wash bowl (a spare, small or collapsible bowl, not your cook pot) from the source. Once filled, move away from the source, and have everyone dip their bandanna into the bowl and use it to clean important areas, starting with the face and ending with the feet. We don't use soap or anything other than water. Pay attention to any "hot spots," or areas in pain due to friction or compression from your pack or shoes. If someone's shoes are hurting their feet, see if you can cut that part of their shoe out to stop the friction or pressure.

Rinse out the bandannas one at a time in the bowl and repeat the process. It can be a real treat to just rinse off the day's sweat, sunscreen, and bug spray as the sun dips below the horizon.

To dump the now-dirty pot of water, do a spinning toss to fan the water out over a large, vegetated area. This is a fun chore for your kids if you think they'll manage to stay dry. Refill the pot as many times as needed to help the whole family get relatively clean. A good clean-up can help prevent unpleasantries such as foot fungus or UTIs (urinary tract infections).

Another option is to dry out wet wipes to save on weight, then when you want to use a couple, you just add water. This does create additional waste to carry out, so we don't do this very often.

We also try to do "laundry" almost every day. Once our kids were potty-trained, we carried two to three pairs of underwear

Rae and Kaleo with their laundry drying on their packs in the Tetons, Wyoming.

and two pairs of socks per person. One pair is what you are wearing, the other pair is what you wore yesterday. Yesterday's pair is dirty, and it's a good time to wash it at the first water source you come to.

Get out your trusty wash bowl, gather some water, move a good distance from the water source, soak your clothing, scrub, and rinse. Repeat till the water runs clear(ish). Hang wet laundry on the outside of your pack to dry during your day's hike, so you'll have clean socks and undies to wear the next day. Sometimes if we don't come to a water source till later in the day, our socks don't have a chance to completely dry overnight. Putting on cold damp socks in the morning is pretty awful, but getting toe fungus would be worse, so we try to adhere to cleaning the socks daily.

Back in the day, jumping into a lake or other water source was a prime way to cool off and clean up after a long day of hiking. People are now realizing the impact that has on these pristine lakes and rivers, so instead they are opting to cool off and clean off a good distance away from the water source to ensure it remains clean and clear for the next generation. I know, it's a bummer, but your great-great-great grandchildren will appreciate it.

NUMBER ONE

When urinating while hiking, make sure to do so at least 200 feet from any water (creek, river, or lake). Go off the trail enough to be out of sight of other hikers. Urinating in the woods is a no brainer if you have male parts. Female parts can be trickier, at least until kids figure out how to lean back. When our daughter was younger, we would pick her up with an arm behind her back and an arm under her knees, so her bum was hanging down, then adjust so she'd be slightly more upright but the urine would still be aimed primarily downward and her pants were out of the line of fire.

Urination devices exist out there to assist in urinating standing up. Do some browsing online. I got my daughter and myself such a device, and talk about a game changer! Not having to expose your bum in mosquito country is awesome. Not having to go far off-trail to find a place to discreetly pop-a-squat is also amazing. Not having to take off my pack every time I have to pee is a bonus.

Some kids (and even adults!) have a bit of trouble peeing in public. To keep things fun and light, Dave developed a term—PWAV (peeing with a view), pronounced *pee wav*—that we've enjoyed introducing to the kids. You rank your view from one to ten with ten being the most amazing thing you've ever seen. The silliness detracts from any awkwardness and has helped our kids learn to relax when they go.

NUMBER TWO

Pooping in the woods can be a hurdle for anyone, even grown-ups. How can we expect kids to handle the tangled precarious balancing act without turning it into a mess? Rest assured, with some practice and patience, your kids can and will master this. One way to get a lot of practice? Go to a restaurant the night before and let your kids have unlimited root beer for the first time in their lives. We made that mistake and were stuck digging holes every hour the next day when one of our kids had major tummy issues. The only good thing about that experience was that it left a major impression on our kids, and they've never had that much soda in one sitting again. Also, now they are total pros at pooping in the woods. Following are some general guidelines.

First, make sure you are at least 200 feet away from any water. Next, dig a cat hole. It should be six inches deep and four to six inches in diameter, which is a pretty big hole and takes time to dig. Look for soft ground near the base of trees. When our kids were toddlers, they didn't give us a lot of notice, so we'd often end up digging a hole after the fact and sliding everything into the hole, including all the messy dirt, and covering it up with dirt that had been taken out of the hole.

If you find that your kids tend to need to poop while you are at a campsite, consider predigging holes when you get to camp so they are ready whenever your child needs to go. Just make sure you fill all holes (used or not) before you leave.

Of course, walking does tend to stimulate the bowels, so there is a good chance they'll have to go "on the go." When ours were very young (back when we had to wipe their bums), we learned that squatting could lead to messes on their pants if they didn't stick their bums back far enough, so we began taking off their pants and underwear completely, or we'd squat/sit in front of them and hold their hands so they could lean far back. Another option is to squat down while holding them in a V shape (one arm under their knees, one arm behind their back, bum down) and let them do their business that way.

You can carry a trowel to make digging easier. We tend to use rocks or sticks found nearby, but it takes a long time to dig, especially if the ground is hard. Carry a sandwich-size bag that holds clean toilet paper, hand sanitizer, and another bag (for used toilet paper). After your kid is done, wipe, then put the used toilet paper in the spare bag, and close it. Sanitize both of your hands, and you're good to go.

Some people prefer to use little water bottle bidets to clean everything. I'm not that coordinated and would probably end up soaking the kids with dirty water streaming down their legs, so we stick to toilet paper. If you do use TP, be sure to pack all dirty toilet paper out with you! Absolutely do not put it in the hole or stick it under a rock. It will not biodegrade before animals in the area dig it up. With dirty paper encased in two bags (one bag for the dirty, which then gets put inside the other bag, which also holds clean toilet paper and hand sanitizer and/or hand wipes), you won't smell it in your pack. You can throw away the dirty TP bag when you get to town or back home. While on the trail, don't burn your TP. The paper tends to fly while burning and can easily start forest fires.

In heavily used areas, you may start to see more requirements to pack out your poop. Some places like Conundrum Creek and Snowmass Lake Trailheads in Colorado's popular Maroon Bells area offer free human waste (WAG) bags and encourage back-packers to take everything out with them. Be sure to research area specific requirements before you head out.

MONTHLY MENSES

Once puberty kicks in, menstruation can cause some people to give up backpacking because it is too much of a messy hassle. Thankfully, by the time this happens, most kids are long past needing help to go to the bathroom, and they'll be able to figure this out too, perhaps with a bit of guidance (and some practice at home).

The two most convenient solutions are tampons and menstrual cups. When I hiked the Pacific Crest Trail, I carried tampons without an applicator (to reduce trash and bulk) in one bag and brought another bag for used tampons. Lining the bag with foil helped make it more discreet and masked the smell. Duct tape around the exterior is another option to help with secrecy, if you don't mind a little added weight. Doubling up your bags or adding a little baking soda can also help with any odors.

In 2012, a report from Kerry A. Gunther, a bear management biologist in Yellowstone National Park, stated that black bears and grizzlies are not attracted to blood, but are curious. Any smells (and that includes your lip balm and toothpaste) could entice them, so use scentless menstrual products and store used and clean products in bear bags at night if you are in bear country. During the day, keep your tampon stash near your bag of toilet paper, so you have toilet paper and hand sanitizer in easy reach. Just toss the waste bag whenever you get to town.

A menstrual cup means less bulk, weight, and waste to carry. Menstrual cups hold blood flow, which you can empty into a cat hole and bury. (It's nice if you can time at least one of the cup emptyings with your daily defecation to eliminate the need to dig extra holes.) If you aren't in a water scarcity situation, you can use water from your water bottle to rinse off the cup prior to reinsertion. Otherwise, toilet paper will do. Boiling the cup can disinfect it. They usually come with little fabric pouches for storage. Keep it in the bear bag when not in use if in bear country.

Encourage your child to practice insertion and use of tampons or cups at home prior to your backpacking trip, as proper fit can be tricky, and you don't want to be dealing with that for the first time out on the trail. If your child seems anxious about how to deal with their period on the trail, take time to present the options. Educating them on the health benefits and hazards of each method can help minimize uncertainty and nervousness at the thought of trying something new.

Whichever method you choose, backup can be nice. Period panties are a great solution. These undies come with flow absorption built into the crotch with minimal bulk added. Just don't rinse them out in streams or other water sources as they may leach chemicals. If you can bring multiple pairs and wait to rinse them in town, that would be best. Panty liners work too, although hiking all day can make it tough for them to adhere properly due to sweat.

I typically don't like pads for backpacking because they are bulky, which takes up extra space in your pack, are more likely to cause chafing, and tend to have a strong odor. But if a full-size pad is all you or your child are comfortable with, then by all means don't let that stop you from getting into the great outdoors. And no matter what method you choose, just remember to store all supplies with other odiferous items inside bear bags and out of the tent at night.

DENTAL CARE

Do not skimp on oral hygiene on the trail. Brushing is just as important in the backcountry as it is at home. A travel-size container of toothpaste works well for shorter trips. If you're going for an extended trip, you may want to pack a second one, but tubes typically last a really long time if you use a small amount.

Brush your teeth as you normally do, using a small amount of water from your bottle. When it comes time to spit, have a hole dug that everyone can spit into, and then cover it up when you're done. Rinse your toothbrushes off over the hole, then suck any remaining water off them and spit that into the hole as well to get the brushes as dry as possible before packing them into your toiletries kit again.

Put your toiletry kit into your bear bag at night if you're in bear country as any fragrance can be an attractor. Put used floss strands into your trash bag. We like to have different color toothbrushes for each person so we don't accidentally use someone else's. All our toothbrushes go into a single toiletries kit that one person carries—this tends to keep our toiletry items organized.

AFTERWORD

The mountains are calling, and now your family is ready to go! Take your time to plan the perfect family backpacking trip, knowing that you will be prepared to handle the chaos and surprises that will inevitably arise during the process. There will be hardships, and there will be incredible beauty. There will likely be giggles that come from mishaps that etch so deeply in your kids' brains that they'll remember the trip for the rest of their lives. And that is what it is about: making those memories and passing down your love of the outdoors to the next generation.

Whether it is your first time leaving home with everything you need on your back or you're a seasoned outdoorsperson who has hiked thousands of miles, backpacking with kids brings another level of magic to the experience. In order to be open to recognizing that magic and not focusing on the bumps in the road, lean on the tricks and tools in this book. Feel free to tear out the whole section on games and take it with you on your first trip or two if you want to have that support. Keep it with the bag

Backpacking with kids is a lot like this picture: it isn't perfect but the memories last forever (and it can sure be pretty). Photo by David Heinrich

of jelly beans in your hip-belt pocket, and bring it out when you need a boost.

As a sleep-deprived mom in the first few years of my kids' lives, the phrase "the days are long, but the years are short" made me want to laugh through my tears. By the time this book comes out, we will have only two more summers with our oldest before she spreads her wings. I feel like I'm on the other end of that parenting timeline, and the years are flying by.

I can confidently say you won't regret any trips you attempt, and how you bounce back from challenges that may arise (and they will!) provides opportunities for your kids to learn resiliency that can't be taught in the comfort of home. Sure, it may take a few months or even a year before you can look back on every trip fondly—we've had our fair share of doozies. But each time something went wrong, it provided us with a stepping stone to level up and improve and adjust for the next trip. I hope that this book will eliminate some of those hiccups and provide a slightly smoother adventure.

Happy trails to you all, wherever you may roam.

Using our umbrellas for shade
on the Superior Hiking Trail, Minnesota.
Photo by David Heinrich

ACKNOWLEDGMENTS

Thank you to my mom for introducing me to hiking and the glory of the outdoors.

Dave deserves awards for planning and preparing all of our adventures and for pushing me to do hard things that are (*almost*) always worth it. Thank you for everything you do to make our lives so epic. I don't have an award to give you, but I can sing your praises to every person who reads this.

Thanks to my kids. This book wouldn't have been possible without you and all our many trips. I can't wait to see where your own paths lead.

Major shout-out to Sarah Gorecki and Casey Blaine at CMC Press who helped me take my chaotic thoughts and get them into a more organized, digestible format. Gretel Hakanson, thank you for your eagle-eye edits. You all are an incredible team!

And to you, intrepid reader, thank you for giving your kids the gift of the great outdoors. I hope for many years of happy hiking for you and your family.

Appendix
YOUR LIGHTWEIGHT SYSTEM

This chart shows some sample weights of gear in three different weight categories. It's easy to see how ounces add up and how the Big Three items (pack, sleep system, and tent) can really have an impact on your total weight. Many smaller online gear manufacturers specialize in lightweight and ultralight gear and are worth exploring when you are cutting weight.

The beautiful thing about gear is that you don't have to be all-or-nothing when it comes to the weight categories path that you choose. We use a quilt that is ultralight but prefer much of the other gear in the lightweight column. However, I would warn you away from carrying gear that is primarily from the traditional column in an ultralight pack. It would be very uncomfortable and likely won't fit.

If you already own traditional gear but are interested in replacing some of it with gear that is more lightweight, I recommend weighing each piece and considering whether to replace it based on the weight savings versus the cost and your budget. If

GEAR	TRADITIONAL	LIGHTWEIGHT	ULTRALIGHT
Pack	**87 oz.** (75 L)	**41 oz.** (68 L)	**9.3 oz.** (62 L)
2-person tent	**62 oz.** (tent with rainfly)	**34 oz.** (single-wall tent)	**16.8 oz.** (tarp)
Sleeping bag/ quilt	**54 oz.** (synthetic mummy bag, 30°F)	**22 oz.** (down mummy bag, 30°F)	**19 oz.** (down quilt, 30°F)
Sleeping pad	**40 oz.** (inflatable, R-value 6.0)	**12 oz.** (inflatable, R-value 4.4)	**10 oz.** (closed foam, R-value 2.0)
Hiking shoes (pair)	**43.2 oz.** (men's size-9 boot)	**31 oz.** (men's size-9 hiking shoe)	**21.4 oz.** (men's size-9 trail runner)
Camp shoes	**52 oz.** (men's size-9 sandal)	**25 oz.** (men's size-9 foam shoe)	**0 oz.** (nothing)
Total weight	**21 lbs. 2.2 oz.**	**10 lbs. 5 oz.**	**4 lbs. 12.5 oz.**

you need gear for your kids, a cost-saving option is to pass your older gear on to them and buy new lightweight gear for yourself. Run a few scenarios and see what combination of gear results in the lightest-weight and most budget-friendly combination for the whole family. Above are examples of weight pathways showing some gear options that could potentially have dramatic weight differences between them.

HELPFUL RESOURCES

These books and websites represent only a tiny fraction of options online. I selected these resources because they are familiar to me, but put lightweight backpacking keywords into your favorite search engine to find even more information. Always be sure to vet your sources and make sure the products or people have experience in the great outdoors. For a list of clickable resources, visit the author's website at maliamaunakea.com /books/backpacking-with-children/helpful-resources.

BOOKS

Andrew Skurka, *The Ultimate Hiker's Gear Guide, Second Edition: Tools and Techniques to Hit the Trail* (National Geographic, 2017)

Christine and Tim Conners, *Lipsmackin' Vegetarian Backpackin': Lightweight, Trail-Tested Vegetarian Recipes for Backcountry Trips, Second Edition* (Falcon Guides, 2015)

Mike Clelland, *Ultralight Backpackin' Tips: 153 Amazing and Inexpensive Tips for Extremely Lightweight Camping* (Falcon Guides, 2011)

Molly Absolon, *Backpacker Magazine's Hiking and Backpacking with Kids: Proven Strategies For Fun Family Adventures* (Falcon Guides, 2012)

Nick Cote, *Wild Eats: Campsite Cooking* (Colorado Mountain Club Press, 2021)

Paul Magnanti, *How to Survive Your First Trip in the Wild: Backpacking for Beginners* (Rockridge Press, 2019)

Ray Jardine, *Beyond Backpacking: Ray Jardine's Guide to Lightweight Hiking* (Adventure Lore Press, 1999)

Richard Louv, *Last Child in the Woods: Saving Our Children from Nature-Deficit Disorder* (Algonquin Books, 2008)

WEBSITES

Trip Planning

AllTrails: Information on various trails, including trail-condition reports by users, *alltrails.com*

CalTopo: Create routes, maps, and check distances and elevations, *caltopo.com*

Columbia River Orienteering Club (CROC): A free, eighteen-part, YouTube series that covers all aspects a modern backcountry person needs to know—in five to ten chunks for easy pacing and self-learning, *youtube.com/watch?v=dl617p5vqu4&list=PLkYHuimd2BspoT35iDNVn-vK6xBsRyhRGA*

Hiking Project: An app with a feature that shows profiles of the trail and where you are on it, *hikingproject.com*

National Climate and Weather Center: Snowpack data, *nrcs.usda.gov/wps/portal/wcc/home*

National Park Service: For planning within National Parks (also check State Parks, Wilderness areas, or any other pertinent websites for your specific trip), *nps.gov/index.htm*

US Topo Maps: Topographic maps produced by National Geospacial Program, *usgs.gov/programs/national-geospatial-program/us-topo-maps-america*

GEAR

Albright Supply: Thin foam pads for sleeping, *albrightssupply.com/ closed-cell-foam-landau-top-padding-1-8-lanpad*8

Cedar Ridge Gear: Quilts, *cedarridgegear.com*

Enlightened Equipment: Quilts, *enlightenedequipment.com*

Gossamer Gear: Ultralight gear, based in the US, *gossamergear.com*

Hyperlite Mountain Gear: Ultralight gear made in the US, *hyperlitemountaingear.com*

Mountain Laurel Designs: Thin foam pads for sleeping, *mountain laureldesigns.com/product/goodnight-eva-1-8-foam-pad*

P Style: Personal urination device, *thepstyle.com*

Purple Rain Hiking Skirts: Tough hiking skirts with big pockets, *purplerainskirts.com*

Ray-Way: Sewing kit and instructions for the first packs I sewed for our kids, *rayjardine.com/ray-way/Backpack-Kit/index.php*

REI: Variety of gear, *rei.com*

Tarp Tent: Lightweight tents made in the US, *tarptent.com*

Thru-Hiker: Sewing kits, materials, and project instructions (this site re-taught me how to sew), *thru-hiker.com/kits*

UGQ Outdoor: Quilts and other gear, *ugqoutdoor.com*

ULA Packs: Lightweight packs made in the US, *ula-equipment.com*

SAFETY INFORMATION

Bear safety: *nps.gov/subjects/bears/safety.htm*

Colorado Mountain Club courses: *cmc.org/education-adventure/ schools-courses*

River crossings: *nps.gov/articles/safe-river-crossings.htm*

Kids' pack weight: *outdoors.org/articles/amc-outdoors/how-heavy-should-my-childs-backpack-be*

NOLS 27 Considerations for a Wilderness First Aid Kit, *blog.nols .edu/2016/06/03/27-considerations-for-a-first-aid-kit*

NOLS Wilderness Medicine and Training: *nols.edu/en/courses*

NOLS Wilderness Medicine Pocket Guide: *store.nols.edu/products/ wilderness-medicine-pocket-guide*

TRAIL FUN

Ilyssa and Dave Kyu, *Campfire Stories Deck for Kids! Storytelling Games to Ignite Imagination* (Mountaineers Books, 2022)

"7 Games to Make Hiking with Kids More Fun": *fatherly.com/play/games-make-hiking-backpacking-kids-fun*

"17 Trail Games and Hiking Activities for Kids and Adults": *coolofthewild .com/trail-games-hiking-activities*

"Trail Games: Activities to Keep Kids Moving and Motivated While Hiking": *outdoors.org/resources/amc-outdoors/adventures/trail-games-activities-to-keep-kids-moving-and-motivated-while-hiking*

ABOUT THE AUTHOR

MALIA MAUNAKEA is a Kānaka Maoli (Native Hawaiian) writer who grew up exploring the trails of Hawai'i before relocating to the continent for college. She writes both middle-grade fiction and nonfiction and is the author of *Lei and the Fire Goddess* (Penguin Workshop, 2023). When not at her computer, she can often be found roaming the Rocky Mountains with her husband, their two children, and a rescue mutt named Peggy. Malia is online at maliamaunakea.com and @MaliaMaunakea on Twitter.

Illustration by Jesse Crock

Join Today.
Adventure Tomorrow.

COLORADO
MOUNTAIN CLUB

The Colorado Mountain Club is the Rocky Mountain community for mountain education, adventure, and conservation. We bring people together to share our love of the mountains. We value our community and go out of our way to welcome and include all Coloradoans—from the uninitiated to the expert, there is a place for everyone here.

cmc.org